100 bright ideas for
BATHROOMS

Tamsin Weston

100 bright ideas for BATHROOMS

BETTERWAY BOOKS
Cincinnati, Ohio

First published in North America in 2003 by

Betterway Books,

 an imprint of F&W Publications, Inc.,

4700 East Galbraith Road

Cincinnati, OH 45236

1-800-289-0963

ISBN 1-55870-630-5

A CIP catalogue record for this book is available from the British Library

Printed and bound in China

10 9 8 7 6 5 4 3 2 1

Contents

Introduction

The bathroom can often be overlooked when it comes to planning and decoration, yet it is a space that is used on a daily basis by the whole family – for getting ready for the day, having a relaxing soak in the bath or perhaps an invigorating and refreshing shower. A bathroom should offer an opportunity for relaxation and tranquillity, so it needs to be a private and peaceful environment for everyone to enjoy.

Planning

Careful planning and research are the key factors in creating a bathroom that's right for you. You need to consider all the options and variations that are available, so you can come up with a plan that suits your needs and requirements, as well as meeting a realistic budget you can work to. It is vital to consider who will be using the room – will it be a busy space for the whole family, or a relaxing peaceful retreat?

It is a good idea to start with a scaled plan to help you work out the exact measurements of your bathroom and hence the space you have available. It is very easy to make a plan of the room yourself using graph paper. Cut out the items (such as a bath, washbasin and so on) that you will be including in your bathroom in scale with the room plan you make. Many bathroom companies feature these scaled plans in their catalogues or can often help you to plan and design a bathroom that suits all your requirements. They will also help you to work out realistic spaces for the areas you are designing – for instance, it is important to allow at least 50cm (20in) of space in front of a washbasin and adequate elbow room on either side. Make sure you note down all the permanent fixtures on your plan, such as doors, windows, radiators and plumbing points. You can then work out how the bathroom features fit and work best within the space you have, trying out different options and variations.

Above left: Ensuring that there is adequate space around the basin will make your bathroom a pleasant and practical place to be in.

Above right: Simple additions, such as a fresh coat of paint or a few shelves, can make a big difference to the feel of your bathroom.

Left: The space available and the positioning of the existing plumbing are key considerations when choosing the fittings for your bathroom.

Bathroom suites

Today there is a huge range of suite options, in different shapes, colours and styles. It is important to choose the right colour as this is the starting point for the rest of the scheme. White is the most popular choice today as it works well with any colour palette, should you decide to change the look of your bathroom in the future. The style can vary hugely too, from period and traditional to cutting-edge contemporary. Suites can be standard and compact, wall hung, back to wall, free standing, or fitted ones which incorporate bathroom furniture.

If you want a clutter-free and streamlined look you might want to choose a suite that includes fitted furniture, as it will help to make use of every available space in the bathroom. Free-standing suites, however, allow you to be slightly more creative and achieve a more individual look. If you have a small bathroom, consider a compact suite, featuring a corner or D-shaped bath, which may give you more space. This is also a good option if a shower is an important feature and you don't have space for a separate cubicle, as a D-shaped bath creates extra space for showering.

Baths come in a range of different materials. Acrylic is one of the cheapest and most popular options today as it is lightweight, practical and retains heat. Cast iron, which is used for roll-top baths, retains heat very well but it tends to be heavy and you may need to reinforce your floor to hold it.

Right: A corner bath is a great space-saving solution and will add a stylish touch to a variety of design styles and colour schemes.

Above: A free-standing bath makes an elegant feature in a spacious bathroom and works well with more traditional design elements, such as tiles or wooden furniture.

Left: If you want to keep the design simple in your bathroom, a conventional rectangular bath is the answer. It can be fitted snugly in an alcove and painted so that it blends into the colour scheme.

Walls

Ceramic tiles are tough and waterproof and ideal for bathroom walls. You can use them sparingly for features such as splashbacks and countertops or make them a key feature by tiling whole areas of walls and floors. There are a multitude of styles – coloured, textured, matt, glossy – and unusual materials such as glass and metal as well. Mosaics are also great choices for bathrooms and create a fresh, stylish, colour coordinated finish which lends itself to contemporary and more unusual schemes. Mosaic tiles come in a multitude of colours and textures and are available singly or in sheets, which can simplify laying them. For a completely individual look, make your own mosaic designs using broken tiles, china or glass for a stunning, unique effect.

Paint is the most popular choice for bathroom walls as it is more durable than wallpaper in a damp area. If you prefer wallpaper, however, try using a vinyl one which will be more water resistant; you can find wallpapers specially designed for use in bathrooms too. An oil-based paint is a good choice for bathrooms as it will resist water and create a seal. However, many paint manufacturers now produce emulsion paints (water-based acrylics) specially formulated for use in damp, moist areas like bathrooms. Anti-condensation paint can be used to treat areas which suffer a damp problem and areas which are prone to steam, such as the walls and ceiling around or above a shower.

The colours you choose for your bathroom depend on the look you want to

Right: Brightly coloured tiles will bring a bathroom to life, creating a fun and stimulating environment for all the family.

achieve – white creates a fresh elegant look that can be combined with practically any other colour. Aqueous, watery shades work wonderfully in bathrooms – use soft aqua or turquoise to create a fresh, cool and calming palette. Bold colours give a vibrant look which is ideal for family bathrooms. Think about combining them with white as bold colours alone can feel heavy, dark and overpowering. Neutral tones, from cream and buttermilk to shades of beige and mushroom, create a stylish, natural feel and should be combined with natural materials for the best effect. Blue and white is another real winner in bathrooms, giving a fresh nautical theme. Combine it with natural wood and soft creamy shades for a slightly warmer touch.

Above left: A tiled splashback is an attractive and practical addition to any bathroom and there are a wide variety of designs and colours to choose from.

Above right: The subtle texture of wooden panels works well with a plain colour scheme and adds definition to the walls.

Storage

Before planning your storage, you need to consider what you actually keep in your bathroom. You may have a whole range of items, including towels, laundry, toiletries and cleaning materials, or you may have just the basic towels and toiletries. Fitted bathroom furniture creates lots of storage and makes the most of available space, but in some bathrooms there is simply nowhere to house any additional furniture. Consider using wall space creatively – for instance, try high-level shelving. Treat dead spaces creatively too; think about fitting shelves or a cabinet in the space at the end of the bath, underneath the bath, or in an unused corner. A false wall, finished with paint, tiles or tongue and groove, can be made to create an extra shelf area.

Above: Make the most of any spare space in your bathroom and make a feature of it in your decorating scheme.

Left: When planning your bathroom, think about how much storage space you will need and which objects will need to be more readily accessible than others.

Right: Rubber flooring makes an unusual alternative to linoleum and works well in a modern-style bathroom.

Below: Wooden flooring looks particularly attractive in a period setting and can be painted to match your chosen colour scheme.

Flooring

Bathrooms need safe, practical, non-slip flooring. It needs to be hygienic, damp resistant and easy to clean. Rubber, vinyl and linoleum floors are a good choice, especially for family bathrooms – they are water resistant, easy to clean, warm underfoot and, most importantly, safe. Natural stone creates a more sophisticated effect and can be found in a non-slip finish. There is a whole range of different styles and colours to choose from, depending on the look and style you wish to achieve.

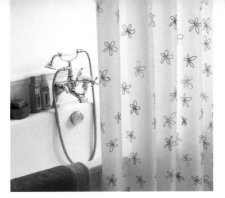

Taps

As well as suites, there's a multitude of taps to choose from. Styles vary from period-style taps to streamlined modern taps. Two single taps are usually found on older suites and lend themselves to more traditional styles. Mixer and monoblock taps have a level control, which allows you to adjust the temperature and flow of water with one hand. These tend to suit modern bathrooms. Don't forget to consider the finish of the tap too – chrome looks wonderful in most bathrooms, while gold and brass are more suited to traditional bathrooms.

Windows

Window treatments are an important aspect of bathroom design and need to be considered carefully as bathrooms often require more privacy than other rooms in the house. There are many different kinds of treatments that bathroom windows can be given. Transparent windows can be replaced with windows that are specially designed for bathrooms and tend to have a more mottled effect. There are many ways to give plain windows a similar effect. Simple roller or Venetian blinds are a simple and unfussy solution and can be adjusted to suit your privacy and the light required at the flick of a cord or pully. There are many products available for creating a frosted sheen to glass – you can be as creative as you like with a patterned stencil effect or, simply cover the whole. Curtains are another option, giving you greater scope in terms of colour, pattern and texture.

Accessories

Accessories can achieve a finished look in your bathroom scheme. Choose them carefully and you can create a styled, themed effect. It's important not to overcrowd the room, however, as there's not usually a great deal of space. Begin with the things that you need, such as towels, bath mats, blinds or curtains, and toiletry bottles. Choose these in materials that work with the feel of the bathroom and the colours on the walls and floors. For example, natural materials such as cotton and linen, wood and stone look great in neutral schemes. Colours are really important too: a nautical theme relies on blue and white as the main colours, but can be complemented with wood or chrome depending on the finish you want to create.

Lighting

Lighting is often overlooked in bathrooms but, carefully chosen, it really helps to create the right effect. For example, if you want a relaxing retreat then the right lighting is vital. Recessed spotlights work well in bathrooms, giving soft pools of light for a relaxing feel when you're soaking in the tub. They can also be used to highlight key areas such as a mirror for shaving and putting on make-up. Dimmers are ideal as you can adjust the lighting to be as bright or as soft as you want it.

Tips and techniques

Here is a quick-reference guide to some of the materials and do-it-yourself (DIY) techniques used in the projects in this book.

MDF

MDF (medium-density fibreboard) is a dense sheet material made from compressed wood fibres. Always wear a dust mask when cutting MDF as the very fine dust is harmful if inhaled over time.

PRIMER

MDF should always be primed before being painted. This step is similar to undercoating wood and stops too much paint being sucked into the MDF as it is painted. You will generally get a better finish when painting wood if you undercoat first, but it is not necessary if you are painting only small areas. If you are painting untreated pine, first seal any knots in the timber with knotting solution. This will prevent the resin from 'bleeding' through the paint and ensure the paint adheres evenly over the wood.

PAINT

Being water-based, emulsion paint is easy to use, dries quite quickly and is easily cleaned off paintbrushes. It is particularly suitable for painting walls. Oil-based paint provides a tougher, moisture-resistant finish. It can be trickier to apply and dries to either a sheen or a gloss finish, but can be more suitable for use in bathrooms, especially on areas that get very wet. Alternatively, there are many paints that are specially formulated for use in damp areas that give a more durable, protective finish.

VARNISH

To protect a decorative finish, an absorbent surface or a water-based paint such as emulsion, use varnish to provide a hardwearing top coat. You will usually need more than one coat of varnish. A clear, matt varnish is ideal. Sometimes you will need a varnish specifically for wood.

Acrylic varnish generally gives a matt finish, while polyurethane varnish gives a much harder, shinier result.

GROUT

All tiles will need grout applied once they have been fixed in place. It is a good idea to use tile spacers to provide an equal distance between each tile.

TILE ADHESIVE

There are various tile adhesives to choose from, including water resistant varieties. Most ceramic tiles require a standard tile adhesive, while floor tiles may need a special adhesive depending on the type of flooring used.

TOOLS

An **electric drill** is an indispensable DIY tool. Most drills come with a set of 'bits' of differing sizes and uses. Match the size of the drill bit to the size of the screw you plan to use. Where you are drilling into a wall, use a masonry bit, which is designed to go through hard surfaces. Insert a wallplug in the drilled hole, then drive the screw into the wallplug. When screwing into wood, the drilled hole should be very slightly smaller than the screw so that the screw grips the wood tightly as it is screwed into place. **Wallplugs** are unnecessary for holding screws in wood.

A **panel saw** is ideal for sawing lengths of wood or MDF. To cut smaller pieces into shape, a **tenon saw** is preferable. A **workbench** with a clamp is useful for making sawing easier.

Bright ideas

Each chapter in this book is divided into the following four sections.

 DONE IN A DAY

Projects requiring some basic DIY skills that you will be able to complete in a day or less.

 QUICK FIX

Instant ideas which are simple to follow and will take less than a morning.

 GOOD IDEAS

A gallery of inspirations for good buys and finishing touches to make a difference quickly.

 GET THE LOOK

Whole decorating schemes for you to recreate and adapt to your own style, with tips on how to achieve the look.

Key to symbols used in this book

Check how long the project will take and how easy it is to do with the at-a-glance guide.

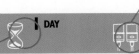

SKILL LEVEL Tells you how easy or difficult the project is.

 HOW LONG Tells you how long the project will take.

You will need
• tape measure
• handsaw
• lengths of 1cm (³⁄₈in) pine board

easy

medium

difficult

Modern bathrooms

The modern bathroom features simple and stylish elements and is fuss-free. There are a multitude of different schemes and effects that can be used to give it a unique look. Splashes of colour, glass, bricks, shiny chrome accessories and simple features are just some of the ideas that will add style to a bathroom. Colourwise, the modern bathroom can be bold and bright with funky touches, or serene and natural, relying on pale muted colours and simple accessories for its key elements.

Chequerboard floor

For a practical flooring that looks great, opt for rubber floor tiles. Simply apply adhesive, or remove the backing for peel-and-stick tiles, then fix to the floor. Non-slip tiles are ideal for bathrooms.

1 Start by drawing a scale plan of your bathroom floor, including permanent features such as the bathroom suite and any additional furniture. Measure your rubber tiles and draw them in position on the scale plan. This will help you to work out the design of the area you are tiling. If the tiles don't fit exactly, you can then decide where to create borders or use cut tiles to fill the space.

⧖ **I DAY**

You will need
- graph paper
- pencil
- tape measure
- hardboard, tape and nails, or levelling compound
- spirit level
- rubber floor tiles
- cutting mat
- craft knife
- metal ruler and set square
- acrylic adhesive
- spatula for adhesive

2 Ensure the surface is flat before you begin. If you have a concrete floor, use levelling compound before you apply the tiles. The levelling compound can also be used as adhesive for the tiles. If the floor is wooden, ensure a level surface by fitting sheets of hardboard over the entire floor. Tape any joins and ensure that the hardboard is securely fixed to the underlying floor.

3 Apply the acrylic adhesive to the floor with the spatula, treating an area the size of a tile. Stick the tile in position and continue with the next tile. When all the tiles are stuck firmly in place, allow the adhesive to dry.

Stencilled bath panel

A coat of paint and a simple stencil on your bath panel will pull your whole scheme together. If you don't already have a wooden bath panel, get a sheet of MDF cut to size.

⏳ **4 HOURS** plus drying

You will need
- MDF panel
- MDF primer
- oil-based paint for panel
- paintbrush
- stencil card
- pencil
- craft knife
- cutting mat
- ruler
- spray adhesive
- oil-based paint for stencil
- stencil brush
- screws
- screwdriver

1 Measure the bath to calculate the panel size needed. Once you have the correct measurements, ask your local DIY store to cut a sheet of MDF to size. Give the panel a coat of primer, then a coat of oil-based paint and allow to dry. Repeat with a second coat.

2 To make a stencil, draw your desired pattern on to stencil card and cut out the shapes using a craft knife. This design is made up of two different stencils, alternated along the length of the panel. Alternatively, buy a ready-made stencil. Use a ruler and pencil to mark the exact position of the stencils.

3 Apply special spray adhesive to the back of the card and position it carefully on the MDF panel. Using a stencil brush, stipple the coloured paint gently over the card. Don't load too much paint on to the brush – it is better to go over it two or three times to build up the depth of colour. Peel off the card and repeat on the next section of the panel, using the pencil marks as a guide.

4 Most baths have a wooden supporting frame or cradle to which you can screw the MDF panel into position. If your bath doesn't have a frame, it is easy to have one made up by a local carpenter.

Simple box shelves

Box shelving has an unfussy, modern look. The shelves can be painted to blend in with your walls or stand out in a contrasting colour.

1 Work out the positions of the shelves and how many you will need, then use a spirit level and pencil to mark out the straight lines on the wall. Cut a timber batten to fit each line, making the batten 12mm (½in) shorter than the line at each end. Drill screw holes at 40cm (16in) intervals along the batten.

2 Hold the batten against the wall with the top level with one of the pencil lines. Push screws through the batten holes to mark the wall behind. Remove the batten and drill holes where you have marked, making them 6mm (¼in) deeper than the wallplugs. Wrap coloured tape around the drill bit to show the correct depth. Measure and drill battens for other shelves in the same way.

3 When you have drilled the wall holes for all the battens, insert wallplugs and secure the battens in place with 6cm (2½in) screws. Use a spirit level to check they are horizontal.

4 Cut pieces of MDF board to make the shelf tops,

4 HOURS plus drying

You will need
- ruler
- spirit level
- pencil
- 3 x 2cm (1¼ x ¾in) timber batten
- saw
- drill
- wallplugs
- coloured tape
- screwdriver
- 6cm (2½in) screws
- 12mm (½in) MDF board
- try-square
- sandpaper
- MDF primer
- oil-based paint
- paintbrush
- 3cm (1¼in) screws
- wood glue
- 4cm (1½in) pins
- hammer
- nail punch

bottoms, fronts and sides. Use a try-square to make sure the corners are square. The depth of the front and side pieces will be twice the thickness of the MDF plus the depth of the battens.

5 Smooth off any chipped edges from the MDF with sandpaper and paint all the shelf parts with MDF primer, then with oil-based paint. Leave to dry.

6 Drill and screw the top piece of each shelf to the wall battens using 30mm (1¼in) screws. Countersink the screw heads so they can be hidden with filler. Repeat with the bottom pieces.

7 Complete the box shelves by gluing then pinning front and side sections on to each shelf using a nail punch. Fill the screw and nail head holes and touch up with paint.

Instant shelving

Use glass blocks to make an easy and stylish storage system. Glass blocks have a cool simplicity that makes them a very versatile home-decorating device. Available in a variety of colours, they look great in bathrooms.

⏳ **| HOUR**

You will need
- glass blocks
- toughened 6mm (¼in) thick sheet glass, cut to size with polished edges
- tape measure
- spirit level

1 Decide where to position your shelves and roughly plan your design. Work out how many blocks you will need to create sturdy supports.

2 To form the shelves themselves, get some sheet glass cut to size at a local builder's merchant – the length should be around 1m (39in).

3 Start to position the blocks for the first shelf. Stand them on the floor, placing them alternately so that they support the front and back edge of the glass shelves. Place the first shelf on top and use a spirit level to make sure that it is perfectly flat.

4 Place the next row of glass blocks on top of the first shelf, again checking with a spirit level and measuring to make sure the blocks are evenly spaced. Repeat for as many shelves as you want.

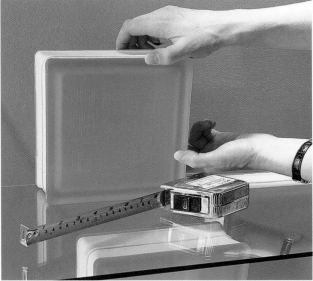

Silver touches

Wall stamps

Draw horizontal lines on the wall using a ruler, pencil and spirit level, and mark out equal spaces where you want the squares to be.

Use a piece of sponge to make the stamp. Draw a square on the sponge with a felt-tip pen and cut out the shape carefully using a scalpel.

2 HOURS

You will need
- ruler
- pencil
- spirit level
- sponge
- felt-tip pen
- scalpel
- silver paint
- plate
- scrap paper

Pour a little of the silver paint on to a plate and dip the sponge into the paint. Practise stamping squares on a spare sheet of paper until you get the hang of the amount of paint and pressure you need. Then stamp squares on to the wall in the positions you have marked. Leave to dry.

Silver wall tiles

Make sure the area you are going to tile is level, clean and free of grease. Apply the tiles to the wall with tile adhesive, starting in the bottom left-hand corner. Work along the bottom row, placing tile spacers between the tiles.

Once you have tiled the first line, use a spirit level to

2 HOURS plus drying

You will need
- sandpaper
- water-resistant tile adhesive
- silver or aluminium tiles
- tile spacers
- spirit level
- tile cutter
- tile grout
- clean, damp cloth

check the tiles are straight and even. Repeat the process until you have covered the area you are tiling. If your tiles don't fit exactly you will need to cut them to size using a tile cutter.

Leave the tile adhesive to dry for 24 hours, then remove the tile spacers and apply grout, carefully working on one tile at a time. Wipe over the tiles with a damp cloth to remove any excess grout and leave to dry.

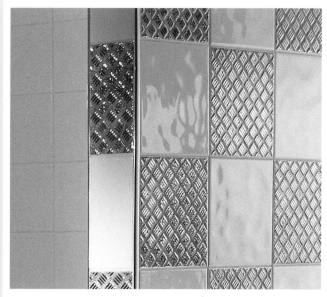

Silver vase

Spread bonding agent on the area of the vase you want to cover with silver leaf. Leave for around 15 minutes, or according to the manufacturer's instructions. Lay the silver leaf on the glue and brush

 30 MINUTES

You will need
- plain vase
- silver leaf kit
- small dry paintbrush
- shellac (if not supplied with kit)

off any excess with a dry paintbrush. When you are happy with the covering, coat the silver leaf with shellac for durability.

Ornate mirror frame

You can use a new or old mirror for this project. If possible, remove the mirror from its frame. If it won't come out, cover the mirrored surface with newspaper and seal with masking tape.

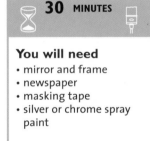 **30** MINUTES

You will need
- mirror and frame
- newspaper
- masking tape
- silver or chrome spray paint

Clean the frame of the mirror to ensure it is free of any grease and dirt and place it on some newspaper. Shake the paint can well and spray the frame with even strokes. For best results, follow the manufacturer's instructions carefully and keep an even distance from the frame when spraying. Leave the frame to dry before replacing it or removing the masking tape from the mirror and hanging it on the wall.

Bright additions

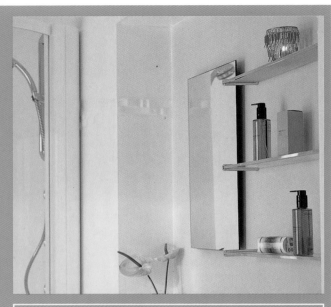

Glass shelving

Transform an alcove or an empty wall with glass shelving and highlight the square of wall around the shelves by painting it a different colour. Mark out your square on the wall using a spirit level, ruler and pencil. Get three glass shelves cut to size, making them at least 25cm (10in) shorter than the width of your square. If you already

⧖ **4 HOURS** plus drying

You will need
- spirit level
- ruler
- pencil
- glass shelves
- masking tape
- coloured emulsion paint
- paintbrush
- shelf brackets
- wallplugs
- drill
- screws
- screwdriver

have glass shelves, mark out the square according to their size, allowing an extra 25cm (10in) of width.

Once you have marked out your square, mask around the area with masking tape. Paint the square using coloured emulsion. Allow to dry and then apply a second coat. Fix up the shelves.

Mosaic alcove

The quickest way to fix mosaic tiles is to use sheets of ready-to-grout tiles. Make sure the walls are free of grease and grime and rub down carefully to ensure that you have an even surface.

⧖ **2 HOURS** plus drying

You will need
- mosaic tile sheets
- sandpaper
- water-resistant tile adhesive
- tile spacers
- white tile grout
- clean, damp cloth

Apply tile adhesive to the backs of the tile sheets. Taking care to line up the sheets properly on the wall, position them carefully and use tile spacers between sheets. Allow the adhesive to dry.

Grout between the tiles, wiping off any excess grout. Once the grout is dry, clean the tiles thoroughly with a damp cloth.

Circles shower curtain

Before you begin, check that the fabric dye pens can be used on the shower curtain. If not, you could use a plain piece of cotton and protect it by sandwiching it between two see-through shower curtains, or two pieces of PVC.

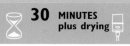

30 MINUTES
plus drying

You will need
- plain fabric shower curtain
- fabric dye pens
- newspaper
- three round objects

Lay the curtain on a flat surface which has been protected with newspaper. Choose three round objects of different sizes to draw round, such as plates or bowls. Draw round the objects with the dye pens to make circles on the shower curtain, overlapping some of the circles.

Finish by colouring in some of the circles to make solid shapes. Allow the dye to dry.

Frosted lantern

Cut out a template of your design from scrap paper. Cover one side of the template with spray adhesive and stick it to the glass. Place the glass on a sheet of newspaper and spray it with frosting spray.

When it is dry, peel off the template. Place the glass on a picture stand and put a tealight behind it. Make sure the flame is far enough away so it doesn't heat up the glass.

15 MINUTES

You will need
- scrap paper
- scissors
- spray adhesive
- glass from a clip frame
- newspaper
- glass frosting spray
- picture stand
- tealight

Chic and sleek chrome

Chrome is sleek and streamlined, perfect for complementing modern bathroom schemes. It can work with bold colours or the simplest muted shades to achieve a stylish, contemporary finishing touch.

▼ Aluminium boxes are perfect for bathrooms as they don't rust. Use them to store bathroom essentials and line them up on shelves for a sleek and tidy look.

▲ A mobile trolley will store towels and they will be within easy reach when you need them.

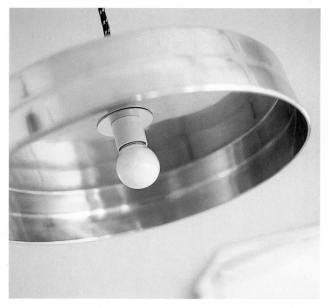

▲ Choose a chrome lamp shade, but if you can't find one, paint one with silver or chrome paint or spray paint.

▲ Add a funky element to your bathroom with curvy chrome and glass shelving units.

▲ A chrome bath rack will help to keep your bathroom tidy and ensure that the items you need on a daily basis are always to hand.

▲ Give a chest of drawers a new look by replacing the handles with streamlined chrome ones.

Make a statement

Use blocks of colour in your bathroom to make a bold statement. Even a plain white bathroom can be transformed with a few areas of bright colour.

▲ Unusual shaped bottles make a quick and inexpensive way of decorating your bathroom.

▼ Make a statement with contrasting colours such as lilac and lime green. Here a bright blind works wonderfully set against a coloured wall.

▲ Choose a fresh blue for your walls to make a bold, modern statement.

▲ Look out for plastic accessories that you can coordinate with your chosen colour scheme, such as dustbins and laundry baskets.

▲ For a contemporary look with colour, keep soft furnishings, towels and accessories to one single colour.

▲ For a dramatic statement, paint your woodwork, ceiling and even furniture in a shade that coordinates with the walls instead of sticking to plain white.

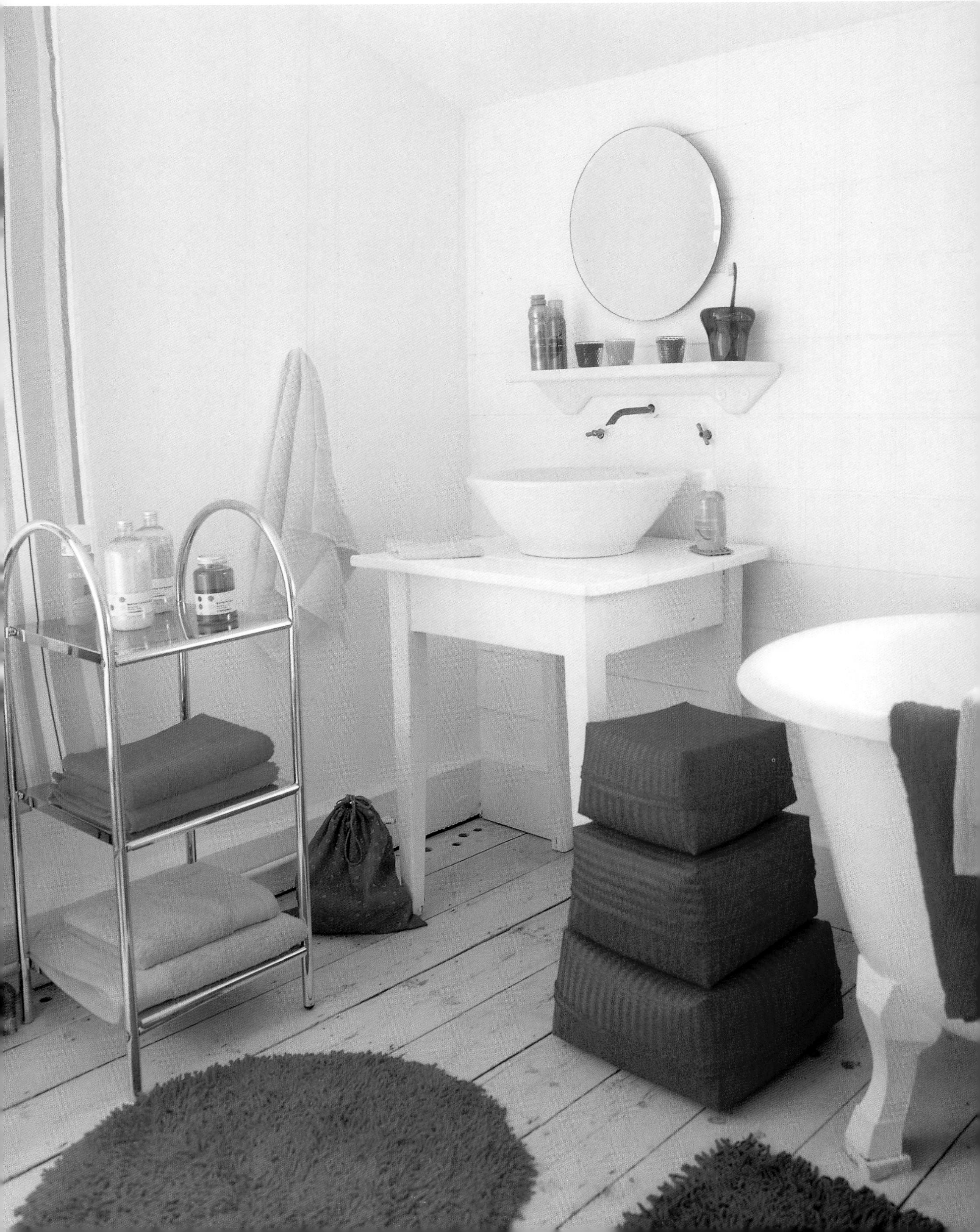

Bright contrasts

Add instant impact to a plain white bathroom with accessories in zingy shades, to be changed when the mood takes you.

This really is a simple and foolproof way to create a splash of colour in your bathroom – great if you're not confident enough to paint the walls with bright colours or haven't the time for serious decoration.

Give the walls a simple finish with white emulsion paint. This could be extended to plain floorboards too, using a gloss paint. This bathroom features a free-standing suite which adds character to the room. Alternatively, a fitted suite would give the bathroom a more contemporary look.

The key to this look is the choice of bold coloured accessories. Bath mats, towels, soaps and bubble baths are great starting points as they can always be found in a good variety of colours. This look will work best if you stick to three or four colours which work together, such as cerise pink, aqua, yellow and blue. Complete the look with chrome accessories for a sleek finish.

What else would work?

- bold coloured bath or bath panel
- brightly painted wooden furniture
- one brightly painted wall

▲ Make an impact by adding bright, zesty towels and bath mats. Clashing colours will give instant drama, so combine shades like cerise pink and aqua.

▲ Make a feature of storage with boxes like these shocking pink ones to keep your room clutter free. Enliven them with a coat of paint to tie in with your colour scheme.

▲ An unusual basin, such as this bowl-shaped one which sits on top of the unit, adds character to this bathroom.

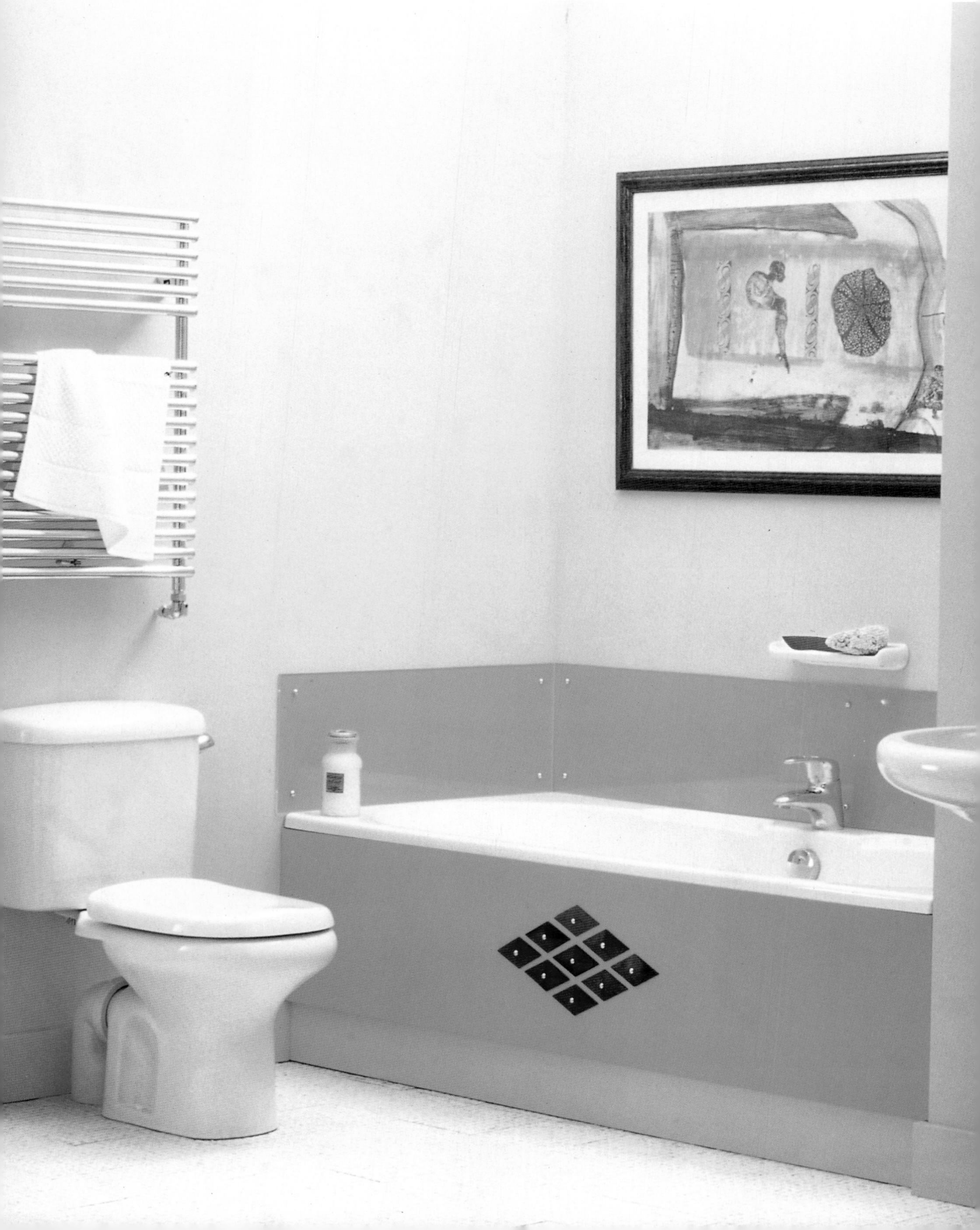

Fresh and elegant

Combine soft aqua with green glass for a stylish bathroom. This simple colour palette gives a fresh, calming and crisp look.

Paint the walls with an emulsion in a subtle aqua shade – this colour creates a lovely calming feel. Green glass is a strong feature here and adds a soothing, reflective quality. Use it to make a splashback and shelving, too. The green becomes stronger once it is placed on the aqua walls. Find a paint colour similar to the green glass and paint the bath panel to match. If necessary, get a sheet of MDF cut to size to make a suitable bath panel.

For a simple decorative effect, stick three-dimensional wooden diamonds on the bath panel using a strong glue. Give these a modern twist by driving a chrome upholstery stud through the centre of each.

Make a feature of a modern radiator and save space by placing it above the bath or toilet. Finally, paint the floor white and add a painting in aqueous shades.

What else would work?

- white, glass or aqua tiles
- natural wood floor
- chrome furniture

▲ For a lovely finishing touch, use clear or soft green bottles and vases that tie in with the other glass features.

▲ Chrome accessories create a stylish finish to this look, giving a sleek and clean effect. Use chrome for the taps, bath rack, shelving and tooth brush holders.

▲ Save space by placing a wall-hung radiator above the bath or toilet.

▲ A simple partition wall creates a convenient alcove for shelving. The glass shelves offer a sleek storage solution and complement the transparent shower front.

▲ A mosaic floor makes an impact and defines the whole look. Get expert help here as the floor needs to be specially prepared.

▲ A smaller size bath makes economical use of the limited space available.

Spa-style bathroom

Use blue mosaics for a dramatic, contemporary space.

The key to this look lies in the mosaic tiles. As well as providing the flooring, mosaic is used in tall columns for impact and for splashbacks behind the shower, sink and shelving. Small areas of the bathroom have been painted – opt for either blue or white to keep the dramatic effect.

This look is ideal for small spaces as it incorporates a shaped bath and shower unit. A corner basin also deals with limited space and the mirror behind it makes the room feel larger. A plain white suite with simple lines is best suited to this look. Windows are kept unadorned in this bathroom, but a simple roller blind in white or turquoise would also work. The simple, uncluttered style of this bathroom means you may need a small amount of furniture or storage to keep the essentials stored away neatly. White furniture would work here, and chrome or aluminium would look great too. Finally, plain purple and white accessories have been kept to a minimum to maintain this fuss-free look.

What else would work?

- applying mosaic to large areas of wall
- gold fittings
- aqua green mosaic tiles

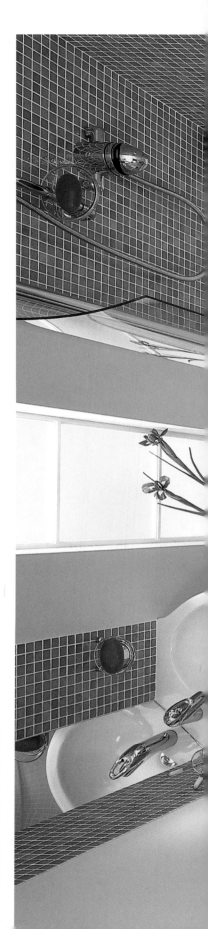

Family bathrooms

The family bathroom should be designed for the whole family to use and enjoy. It needs to be practical, functional and stimulating to make bath-time fun. Generally, bright and vibrant shades work best, to create a stimulating environment for children. Practical features are key, and careful consideration needs to be given to the materials you choose. Practicality aside, there is huge scope for fun – give the bathroom a theme and work with bold colour for instant impact.

Mosaic table top

Add colourful decoration to a plain table or cabinet top with handmade mosaic tiles.

1 Wrap the ceramic tiles in a towel and gently knock them with a hammer. Alternatively, use tile nippers to create shards of varying sizes.

2 Lay out the broken pieces on the surface you want to cover and move them around until you are happy with the arrangement.

3 Working from one edge, use a notched spreader to create an even layer of tile adhesive over a small section of the surface. Position the pieces of tile on top and press lightly into the adhesive. Work in small sections until you have covered the whole area.

⏳ **4 HOURS**
plus drying

You will need
- ceramic tiles
- towel and hammer or tile nippers
- tile adhesive with notched spreader
- piece of wood or MDF
- tile grout
- squeegee
- damp cloth

4 Press a piece of wood or MDF evenly on top of the tiles to ensure the surface is level, and remove any excess adhesive with the spreader. Leave the adhesive to dry thoroughly, following the manufacturer's instructions.

5 Once dry, fill the spaces between the tiles with grout using a squeegee and wipe the tiles clean with a soft, slightly damp cloth. Leave to dry.

Duckling shower curtain

Give your bathroom a fun duckling theme using clear plastic accessories.

⏳ **4 HOURS**

You will need
- coloured picture of a duckling
- scissors
- 2 pieces of PVC, each the size of a shower curtain
- clear-drying glue or double-sided sticky tape
- sewing machine
- eyelet kit
- shower curtain hooks

1 To begin, find a colour photograph or picture of a duckling (try looking in an animal or farmyard book). You'll then need to get this colour photocopied as many times as you want to use the image, to a suitable size. You can try variations in the pattern, such as one large image or a single row or panel of smaller images.

2 Cut out the duckling shapes and arrange them in a pattern on one of the pieces of PVC, allowing space at the top for eyelets. Stick them down when you are happy with the design.

3 Place the second piece of PVC over the top and use a sewing machine to sew the two pieces together around all four edges, again leaving a border at the top for the eyelets. This will prevent the images from getting wet.

4 Fix the eyelets along the top of the curtain above the stitched line and add hooks to attach to a shower curtain rail.

Instant splashback

Perspex makes a great splashback – it fits over existing
tiles and allows you to sandwich paper motifs in between.

3 HOURS
plus drying

You will need
- 2 pieces of Perspex to fit the splashback
- drill
- tracing paper
- pencil
- coloured paper
- craft knife
- cutting mat
- spray adhesive
- 4 mirror screws
- screwdriver
- clear silicone sealant

1 Place one piece of Perspex on top of the other and line them up carefully. Drill four holes through both pieces, one in the middle of each side. Then drill matching holes in the tile splashback.

2 Copy some butterfly motifs on to tracing paper, then transfer them to the coloured paper and cut out carefully with a craft knife.

3 Arrange the motifs on one sheet of Perspex. When you are happy with the design, spray the motifs with adhesive and stick on the Perspex.

4 Place the second piece of Perspex on top and fix the whole splashback in place with mirror screws. Seal the joins with sealant to stop the inside misting up.

Three-toned walls

This subtle effect, using three different shades of the same colour, will add a new dimension to your walls.

1 Make sure the walls are clean of grease and grime. Choose the areas of wall to paint, divide the height into three and mark each third of the wall with a pencil. Use a ruler and spirit level to ensure the lines are straight and even.

2 Working from the bottom up, apply masking tape carefully above the first line, in order not to paint the wrong area. Make sure you apply the tape as straight and evenly as possible.

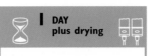

⏳ **1 DAY plus drying**

You will need
- long ruler
- spirit level
- pencil
- masking tape
- 3 tones of one matt emulsion paint colour
- paintbrush or roller

3 Paint the area below the bottom line with the darkest shade. Allow to dry and apply a second coat if needed.

4 Once the paint is dry, carefully peel off the masking tape. Now apply masking tape above the second line and below the first line and paint the area in between with the middle shade. When dry, remove the tape and apply tape below the second line. Paint the top section in the lightest shade and remove the tape when dry.

Colour transformations

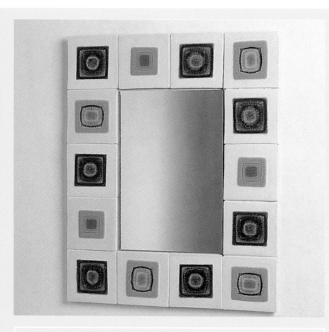

Tiled mirror frame

This frame looks best if you only use complete tiles, so try to find a mirror that has the right dimensions for your tiles.

Drill holes in the wall to match those in the corners of the mirror, then screw the mirror on to the wall above the washbasin.

⧗ **2 HOURS** plus drying

You will need
- mirror
- drill
- screws
- screwdriver
- tile adhesive
- tiles
- tile spacers
- tile grout
- clean, damp cloth

Carefully spread a layer of tile adhesive down one edge of the mirror. Arrange the tiles along the edge of the mirror on the adhesive, using tile spacers to separate them. Repeat this process around the other three sides of the mirror. Leave to dry.

Once dry, remove the tile spacers and apply grout between the tiles. Wipe off any excess grout with a damp cloth and allow to dry.

Flower shower curtain

Lay the white cotton on a flat surface protected by newspaper or polythene. Use the fabric marker pens to draw simple flower outlines on to the cotton, or alternatively make a simple template to create the motifs. If necessary, draw over the lines again to get an even effect. Leave to dry. You may need to iron the fabric to fix the dye – make sure you follow the manufacturer's instructions.

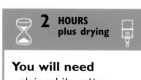

⧗ **2 HOURS** plus drying

You will need
- plain white cotton
- newspaper or polythene
- fabric marker pens
- 2 pieces of PVC or transparent shower curtains
- curtain clips and shower curtain hooks

Sandwich the cotton curtain between the two pieces of PVC for protection. Attach clips and hooks to all three layers and hang on the shower curtain rail.

Painted duckboard

Ensure the duckboard is clean and dry. Stand it on newspaper and apply a coat of wood primer, then allow to dry.

Using an oil-based paint, carefully paint the top of the duckboard and leave to dry. Next paint around the edges of the duckboard and leave to dry.

Give the top a second coat and, once dry, give the edges a second coat.

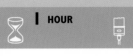

45 MINUTES
plus drying

You will need
- unfinished wooden duckboard
- newspaper
- wood primer
- paintbrush
- oil-based paint

Instant privacy

Translucent paper is ideal for discreetly blocking overlooked windows where extra privacy is needed. Use colours that coordinate with your room scheme, or add a bright pattern.

Measure your window panels and cut shapes of tracing paper or other translucent but not see-through paper to fit the panels. Make spots by drawing round an eggcup or a similar round object on to coloured papers, then neatly cut out the spots.

Cut a template from plain paper to fit the windows and draw a grid on it with a ruler and pencil. Lay one of the tracing paper panels over the template and use the grid to position the coloured dots. Stick them in position and repeat with the other panels. Spray the back of each panel with adhesive and stick to the window panes.

1 HOUR

You will need
- ruler
- tracing paper
- eggcup
- coloured papers
- pencil
- plain paper
- spray adhesive

Handles and hooks

Mosaic toilet roll holder

Either leave one tile's gap when you are tiling the wall or carefully remove a tile from an already tiled wall. Cut a square from the sheet of mosaic tiles large enough to fit the hole. Use tile adhesive to stick the sheet of tiles in the gap and allow to dry.

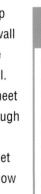

⏳ **2 HOURS** plus drying

You will need
- sheet of mosaic tiles
- craft knife
- tile adhesive
- tile grout
- pencil
- masking tape
- drill
- toilet roll holder
- screwdriver

Grout between the tiles and allow the grout to dry. Mark the place on the mosaic tiles where you need to drill a hole to fix the toilet roll holder in place. Stick a piece of masking tape over the tile you are going to drill, to prevent it cracking. Drill the hole and screw the toilet roll holder into place.

Stone door handle

Sand down the base of the pumice stone to ensure it is as flat as possible. Apply some glue to the flat surface and stick it on to the door knob. Hold securely in place and leave to dry.

⏳ **45 MINUTES**

You will need
- pumice stone
- sandpaper
- strong glue
- flat door knob
- pencil

Mark the position on the door where you want the door handle to be and fix it into place. This handle could also be used on a cupboard.

Seaside drawer knobs

Remove the old handles from a chest of drawers and lightly sand down the wood. Paint the chest in a nautical shade to match the handles you have chosen, applying more than one coat if necessary. Allow the paint to dry.

⧖ **2** HOURS plus drying	
You will need	
• sandpaper	
• oil-based paint	
• paintbrush	
• ruler	
• pencil	
• seaside-themed door knobs	
• screwdriver	

   Measure and mark the positions of the new drawer knobs on the chest and screw them into place.

Decorative towel hooks

Use a ruler and pencil to draw a line on the wall or door where you want to fix the knobs. Use a spirit level to check the line is horizontal. Measure out the exact positions of the knobs, spacing them equally along the line. Use a screwdriver to fix the knobs to the wall or door.

⧖ **30** MINUTES	
You will need	
• ruler	
• pencil	
• spirit level	
• glass door knobs	
• screwdriver	

   It is a good idea to give each member of the family their own hook by using a selection of different door knobs.

▲ Plastic storage units are cheap and practical and give a sense of continuity among other plastic accessories.

Colour shock

The plainest bathroom can be jazzed up using brightly coloured accessories. To keep the look simple and bold, choose just two or three shades to work with.

▼ If you have a small bathroom, make use of every available space, including the back of the door. Hang a drawstring bag on a hook to hold your laundry, as well as hanging towels here too.

▲ Fill plain glass bottles with coloured bubble baths to coordinate with your scheme.

▲ Rubber is great for bathrooms as it grips well and can be non-slip. If you are short on space, use suction pads on your tiles to hold toiletries in place.

▲ Customize storage jars to coordinate with your colour scheme or add a contrasting splash of colour.

▲ If you can't afford storage furniture or don't have much space, plain boxes can be jazzed up to make cheap and efficient storage. Use paint or coloured paper to cover them and stick labels or tags on the front of each box so you know exactly what's inside.

Funky combinations

Use bold colour combinations to create a fun, bright and stimulating bathroom for the kids.

▲ Painting a striking mural on to tiles with tile paint creates a colourful stimulating environment for children; they can even join in with the painting.

▼ A cheap and quick way to add colour in the bathroom is to dye your towels. You could even stick name labels on to them for a personal touch.

▲ Coloured tiles are a great starting point for adding colour – they can be placed randomly or in a pattern.

▲ Make bathtime fun with coloured soaps. These are a cheap way of adding a decorative element.

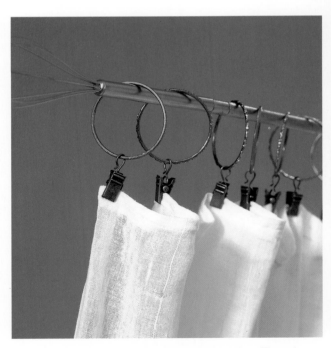

▲ Swap curtain rings for colourful bangles. Thread them on a curtain pole and clip to the curtain with curtain clips. Alternatively, stitch the bangles directly to the curtain fabric.

▲ Customize soft furnishings in the bathroom with playful patchwork motifs. Cut out squares from coloured fabrics and sew them on to laundry bags and storage pockets. It's great fun to make them personal by cutting out children's initials and ages.

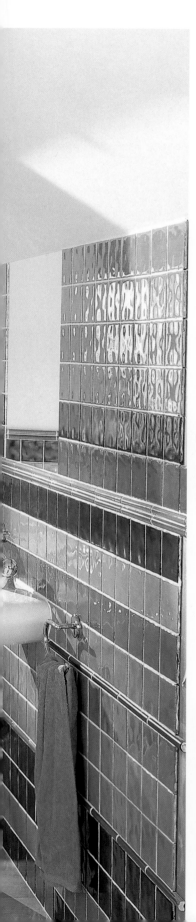

Technicolour tiles

Use bands of brightly coloured tiles to create a stimulating, technicolour bathroom.

This colourful style can be applied to the plainest white bathroom, starting with neutral white walls. This look works best with one or two tiled walls, as any more may be too much. Once you have worked out how many tiles you need and the area that you are going to cover, choose up to four different vibrant shades of tiles, such as blue, yellow, red and purple. Apply the tiles in horizontal lines of colour.

For a really bright look you could even choose flooring in another shade. This bathroom features wood laminate flooring – the most practical choice to achieve a similar look is to go for a wood-effect vinyl flooring as real wood is not really suitable for very damp areas.

Fit a blind that coordinates with the tiles – a navy blue or yellow, perhaps. This is a colourful bathroom so a white bathroom suite is the best choice to set off the tiles. If you want to add shelving, display a few colourful objects to emphasize the theme.

What else would work?

- a coloured suite to match the tiles
- random patterns of tiles or vertical lines
- coloured walls

▲ This innovative shelving unit makes good use of an otherwise redundant space and helps to separate the bath area from the rest of the room.

▲ Choose a modern coloured blind to create extra impact. Select a colour that coordinates with your tiles.

▲ Fake flowers are a quick and easy way to add colour and give the bathroom a fun element.

Marine style

Use shades of aqua and mosaic to create a smart, practical family bathroom. The simplest way to create the mosaic effect is to use a water-resistant wallcovering.

This cheerful bathroom scheme creates a stimulating atmosphere and the mid-aqua walls give the room a fresh vibrancy.

For practicality and durability, PVC (vinyl resin) floor tiles have been used in a similar shade to work with the rest of the scheme. For added impact, the flooring incorporates a slightly sparkly quality.

To protect the painted walls, it may be worth putting up a simple glass or Perspex splashback along the length of the bath, especially if your children are young.

Shelving is kept at a sensible height, out of reach of small children. A mosaic wallcovering has been used to jazz up an old cabinet, as well as lining shelf edges for an added decorative touch. Try using real mosaic panels as insets between plain white tiles to further enhance the look. Finally, keep accessories to a minimum for this breezy look.

What else would work?

- rubber or stone floor tiles
- chrome accessories
- brightly painted walls with mosaic borders or panels

▲ Glass shelves work well in an aqua bathroom as they enhance this clean, fresh look, as well as blending in beautifully with the colour scheme.

▲ The mosaic features in this bathroom are easy to create. The cupboard, shelf and the edge of the bath have been covered with water-resistant paper.

▲ Mosaic tiles interspersed with plain white ones create a colourful splashback.

Natural style

A natural-look bathroom creates a **soft** and **calm** oasis using a combination of natural materials and colours. This style is easy to achieve and can be **modern, pared down** and fuss-free, or slightly more **traditional** and **cosy**. Choose materials such as **stone**, wood, **bamboo**, cotton, **linen** and rattan – these rustic elements provide a warm, finished look.

Decorative window grille

Create an unusual window treatment for a non-opening window using decorative MDF or an old radiator screen. Paint it in a neutral shade to coordinate with your scheme.

1 Measure the window carefully and get a sheet of decorative MDF cut to size. Alternatively, if you are using an old radiator screen, cut it to fit the dimensions of the window.

2 Make sure the screen is clean, dry and free of grease, then paint it using MDF primer and allow to dry. Next apply a coat of oil-based paint. Make sure you apply paint to all the nooks and crannies. Once the first coat of paint is dry, apply a second coat and allow to dry.

3 Drill a hole in each corner of the screen and screw to the window frame. If you have a recessed window, you could fasten the screen to the front of the recess, flush with the walls.

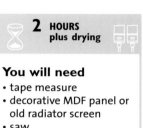

2 HOURS
plus drying

You will need
- tape measure
- decorative MDF panel or old radiator screen
- saw
- MDF primer
- paintbrush
- oil-based paint
- drill
- screws
- screwdriver

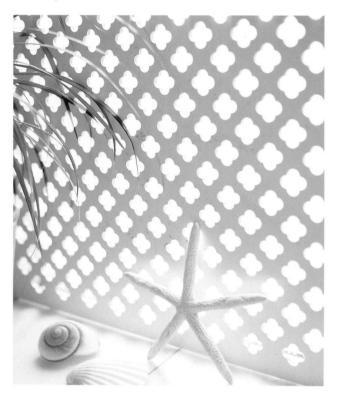

Glass washbasin stand

Convert a simple self-assembly kitchen trolley into a stylish washstand with the addition of an elegant glass washbasin and towel rail.

1 If two of the trolley's legs are shorter than the others (to allow for castors), cut the longer legs down so they are all the same length. Assemble the trolley according to the instructions, but don't attach the top.

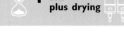

DAY
plus drying

You will need
- self-assembly kitchen trolley
- saw
- glass washbasin
- pencil
- pair of compasses
- ruler
- drill
- jigsaw
- sandpaper
- spade bit
- woodstain
- paintbrush
- quick drying clear varnish
- taps
- waste pipe and collar
- stainless steel towel rail
- wood drill bit
- screws
- screwdriver

2 Centre the glass bowl upside down on the underside of the trolley top. Draw around it with a pencil. Then use a pair of compasses and a pencil to draw another circle about 6cm (2½in) in from the first, so that about one-third of the basin will sit beneath the

trolley top. Drill a hole inside the pencil line to take the jigsaw blade and carefully cut out the smaller circle. Smooth any rough edges with sandpaper and try the basin in the hole for size.

3 Decide where you want to position the taps, making sure they don't interfere with the structure of the trolley. Drill holes through the wooden trolley top for them, using a spade bit. Stain the trolley all over with woodstain and leave to dry. Finish with a coat of varnish and allow to dry.

4 Attach the top panel to the washstand. You may need a plumber to fix the bowl in place using the collar, and plumb in the water supply and waste pipe. Finish by attaching the towel rail to the front of the stand.

Mosaic wall

Mosaic tiles in neutral tones create a soft, textured effect on walls and other surfaces.

I DAY
plus drying

You will need
- plumbline
- pencil
- ruler
- tile adhesive with spreader
- mosaic tile sheets
- tile spacers
- craft knife or scissors
- tile grout with spreader
- clean, damp cloth
- dry cloth

1 Make sure all surfaces are clean and even. Using a plumbline, pencil and ruler, mark a vertical line in the centre of the wall, from which you will begin fixing the tiles, working from the centre of the wall outwards towards the corners.

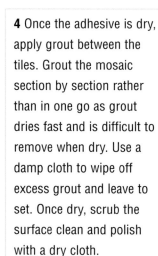

2 Use the notched adhesive spreader to apply a thin bed of adhesive to the wall, covering an area the size of the first sheet of tiles. Keep the spreader's notches in contact with the wall, and you are guaranteed a consistent 3mm (⅛in) thick coating.

3 Fix the first sheet of tiles to the wall. Use plastic tile spacers between sheets to make sure that the gaps are consistent. Work your way out from the centre to the corners of the area you are working on. Work section by section so that the adhesive doesn't dry out in areas where you haven't yet laid tiles. You can cut tile sheets to fit recesses and spaces at the edges of the walls and lay them in the same manner.

4 Once the adhesive is dry, apply grout between the tiles. Grout the mosaic section by section rather than in one go as grout dries fast and is difficult to remove when dry. Use a damp cloth to wipe off excess grout and leave to set. Once dry, scrub the surface clean and polish with a dry cloth.

Rustic panelling

Transform a plain wall with elegant tongue-and-groove wood panelling treated with a subtle paint effect.

1 Measure the wall to calculate the area of tongue and groove you need and get it cut to size or cut the planks yourself.

2 Lay some newspaper on a flat surface and place the planks on top. Apply a coat of matt emulsion or woodwash to the planks, depending on the effect you want to create. A woodwash gives a light coverage, allowing the grain to show through. This effect can also be achieved by watering down matt emulsion paint. Allow the first coat to dry before applying a second coat, if necessary. Leave to dry.

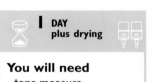

DAY plus **drying**

You will need
- tape measure
- pencil
- ruler
- saw
- tongue-and-groove panelling
- newspaper
- matt emulsion or woodwash paint
- paintbrush
- 2.5cm (1in) softwood battening
- spirit level
- drill
- 5cm (2in) screws
- screwdriver
- wallplugs
- 2.5cm (1in) panel pins
- hammer
- small wood offcut
- nail punch
- wood filller
- sandpaper
- moulding or shelf

3 Attach the battens horizontally to the wall to support the tongue and groove. You will probably need three rows of battens. Mark out their positions about 40cm (16in) apart, checking with a spirit level that they are horizontal. Drill holes through the battens at about 30cm (12in) intervals, hold them up against the wall and mark the positions for the drill holes. Drill the holes in the wall as marked, and insert wallplugs. Screw the battens to the wall.

4 Measure and mark out where the tongue-and-groove planks will go. Position the first against the wall, with

the tongue facing away from the direction in which you are going to work. Check it with a spirit level. Nail the plank to the battens using panel pins. Slide the next board up against the first and gently tap in place with a hammer, using an offcut of wood to protect the board's edge. Nail it in place. Repeat to cover the wall.

5 Punch in the pin heads below the surface of the wood. Fill in the pin holes with filler and sand smooth. Touch up with paint. Finish with moulding or a shelf along the top.

Natural-style storage

Hessian paint kettles

Paint kettles make roomy storage for soaps and other accessories. Cut a strip of hessian the depth of the kettle and long enough to fit all the way round. Remove a few threads from each edge of the rectangle to leave an attractive frayed edge. Glue the hessian to the kettle and allow to dry. Use a length of raffia to tie a brown card label in place to finish.

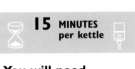

15 MINUTES
per kettle

You will need
- paint kettle
- hessian
- scissors
- strong glue
- raffia
- label

Bathroom storage unit

First paint the units with matt emulsion. Allow to dry and add another coat if necessary.

Remove the drawers and drill holes in the backs of the units, roughly where the two middle drawers go. Hold the central unit in position, checking it is level with a spirit level, and mark the points on the wall for drilling.

Drill the holes in the wall, insert wallplugs and screw the first unit in position. Repeat with the other units. If you prefer open shelves, simply leave out the drawers.

4 HOURS
plus drying

You will need
- unfinished storage boxes with drawers
- neutral matt emulsion paint
- paintbrush
- drill
- spirit level
- pencil
- wallplugs
- screws

Mini cabinet

Measure and cut the plywood shelf to fit across the box frame. Sand the edges to make them smooth. Paint the box frame and shelf with a coat of primer, then two coats of paint and allow to dry.

Once the frame is dry, measure and cut a piece of wallpaper to fit the back of the frame and stick in place. Fix the plywood shelf in position using small brackets and screws.

HOUR plus drying

You will need
- box frame (you could make one from MDF)
- plywood for shelf
- sandpaper
- wood primer
- oil-based paint
- paintbrush
- wallpaper
- ruler
- pencil
- scissors
- adhesive
- 2 small shelf brackets
- screws
- screwdriver

Handy wall storage

Make the most of the space at the end of the bath by adding a storage unit. Measure the space carefully before buying the unit to make sure it will fit.

Drill four screw holes in the back of the unit, two at the top and two at the bottom. Mark the position of the holes on the wall, using a bradawl or pencil.

Drill the holes in the wall where you have made the marks and insert wallplugs. Screw the unit to the wall.

HOUR

You will need
- storage unit
- drill
- bradawl or pencil
- wallplugs
- screws

A touch of nature

Painted flower panels

Trace around a leaf or flower motif, copy it on to thin card and cut out.

Measure and mask off three equal rectangles above the bath. Paint the rectangles with green paint and leave to dry. Mask off a smaller panel inside each rectangle.

Spray adhesive on to the backs of the motifs and stick one in each panel.

Paint the smaller rectangles with white paint using a roller, painting straight over the motifs. Leave to dry. Peel away the card and remove the tape.

 2 HOURS plus drying

You will need
- leaf or flower motif
- tracing paper
- pencil
- thin card
- scissors or craft knife and cutting mat
- tape measure
- masking tape
- green paint
- roller
- spray adhesive
- white paint

Scented herb sachets

Cut two rectangles of organza, about 15x10cm (6x4in). Sew them together, leaving one end open to make a small sack. Turn through the right way and fill the bag with dried herbs such as lavender and rosemary. Tie with a ribbon to coordinate with the fabric and place in drawers to scent your clothes or linens.

⏳ **20** MINUTES per bag

You will need
- organza fabric
- scissors
- sewing machine or needle and cotton
- dried herbs
- ribbon

Embroidered curtain panel

Measure the length of the panel curtain and cut one or two strips of embroidered fabric to the same length and around 15–30cm (6–12in) wide. Remember to leave a little extra around all sides for a hem.

I HOUR

You will need
- plain panel curtain
- tape measure
- embroidered fabric
- pencil
- scissors
- needle and cotton or iron-on hem tape

Neatly hem the edges of the embroidered fabric using either a needle and cotton or iron-on hem tape. Pin, then sew the embroidered panels to the curtain, making sure they hang straight.

Alternatively, you could add one horizontal strip of embroidered fabric at the bottom of the panel curtain.

Bamboo curtain

Cut three pieces of bamboo cane to the width of the window and bind them together at both ends with garden twine. Cut several more canes to the length of the window, less about 7.5cm (3in) to allow for the twine.

3 HOURS

You will need
- bamboo canes
- small saw or craft knife
- garden twine
- masking tape
- hand drill
- 2 screw-in hooks

Stick a small piece of masking tape around one end of a bamboo cane to prevent it splitting. Using a hand drill, make a hole all the way through the cane and remove the tape. Repeat with the other canes.

Take two bamboo canes and thread a length of twine right through the holes in both of them. Knot at both ends, leaving about 10cm (4in) of twine between the canes. Pair up the remaining canes in the same way.

Screw two hooks into the window frame and fix the three-cane pole in position. Hang the twine over the pole with a cane on either side and spread them out evenly.

Pure style

Add simple elements in a limited colour palette for a pure and serene bathroom. Glass jars, natural tiles and a few easy finishing touches, such as plants and pebbles, are all you need.

▲ Grasses grown in a slim white window box bring a touch of nature indoors, complementing natural materials and pure white schemes.

▼ Simple glass jars will hold a whole bag of cotton wool balls and similar items, so you won't need to fill a cupboard with odds and ends.

▲ Use simple tin containers for storage. You can even make them yourself from sheets of perforated tin, or add small decorative pieces of tin to plain cans.

▲ Some plants really enjoy the humid warmth of the bathroom. Choose a plant pot that fits the colour scheme.

▲ Restrict the colours you use, mixing and matching with just a few neutral shades. Interest can be introduced in the form of different textures, such as mosaic tiles.

▲ Canvas is a wonderful and inexpensive natural fabric and can be used for soft furnishings and items such as laundry baskets.

Rustic

Rustic accessories made from natural materials make wonderful finishing touches in the bathroom. Rattan, wicker, wood and bamboo all add texture and interest.

▼ A sturdy laundry basket can double up as a seat when topped by a padded cushion.

▲ Use a wicker shopping basket to store towels or toiletries. Bring wood into your bathroom in small touches, such as a wooden duckboard.

▲ The straw-covered candles add texture in this natural scheme, as do the wooden soap dish and bath rack. A small chest with lots of drawers makes great storage for cleaning products, soaps and make-up.

▲ This chest combines a smart wood shell with woven baskets as deep, practical drawers.

▲ Shopping baskets or garden trugs make great storage for towels and toilet rolls.

▲ Wicker, rattan and wood work wonderfully together, to create a variety of textures. Ali Baba baskets enhance the rustic feel with their soft curves.

Natural materials

Accessorize your bathroom with the soft, subtle tones of natural materials. Use natural woods, plain ceramics and stone accessories along with pure white or cream towels to achieve this look.

▲ Mix different materials together to create an interesting feel. Here, a stone storage jar brings the scheme together.

▼ Fill empty Kilner jars with bath salts and add fresh herbs and a few drops of scented oil. Tie bunches of herbs and eucalyptus and use to add a natural fragrance to the room.

▲ Wooden wine boxes make stylish, practical storage. They stack easily and can be picked up free from a local wine merchant.

▲ Fill a wooden bath rack with natural bath products to enhance the feel. The wood has been painted white for a more subtle effect.

▲ A straw mat, wicker laundry basket and wooden accessories add to the old-fashioned style of this free-standing bath.

▲ A large fluffy towel makes an attractive laundry bag. Fold in half and sew up the two sides to create a bag. Hem the top edge to create a channel and thread with thick cord to make a drawstring top.

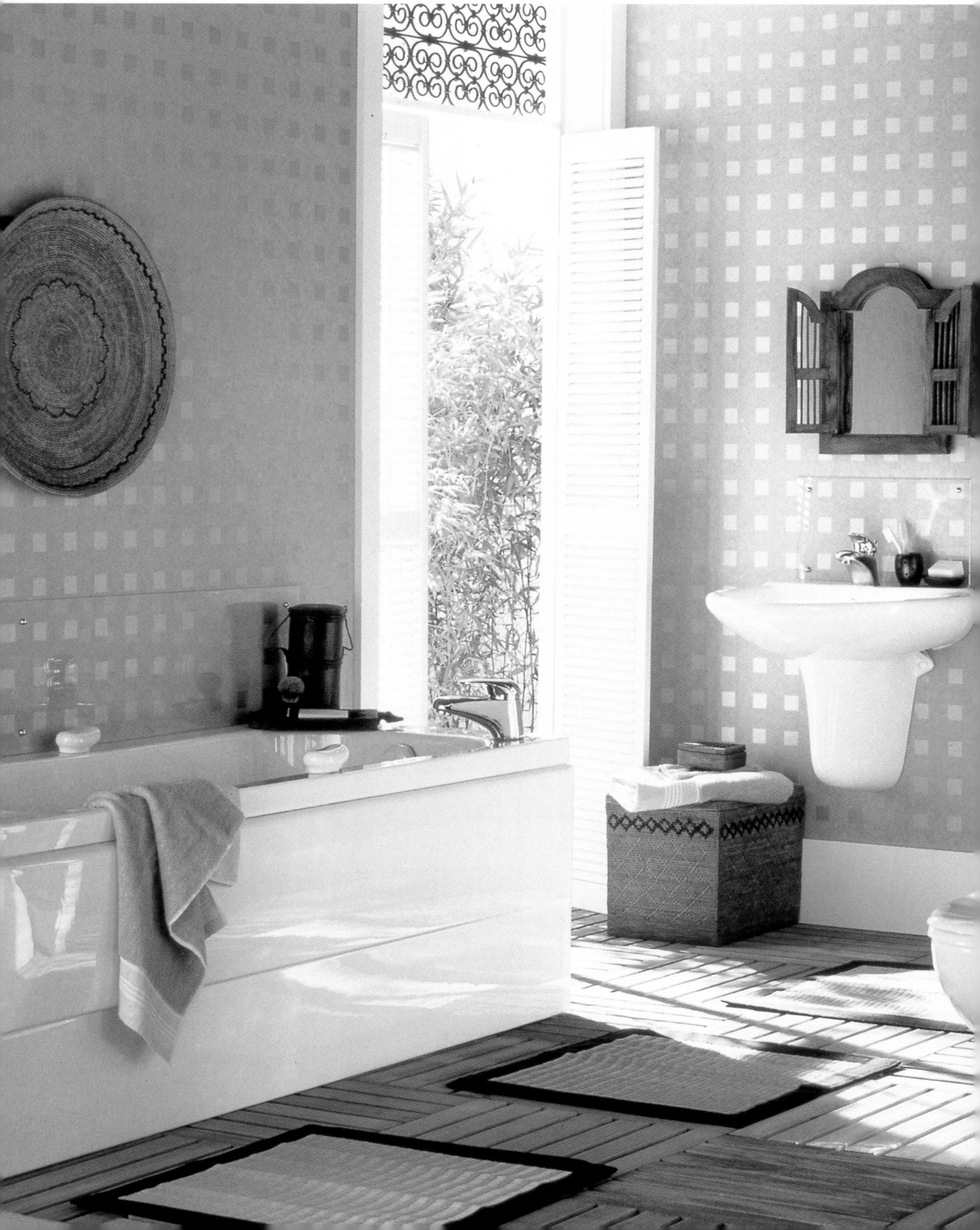

East meets west

Combine neutral tones and natural materials to create a stylish Oriental bathroom.

This neutral colour combination is hard to get wrong. Choose a pale mushroom colour for the walls and create a chequerboard effect using a simple square stamp and some pale, metallic gold paint. Alternatively, you could use a decorative pattern, but apply it more sparingly.

This bathroom features decking, a clever and effective way of covering the floor. Decking tiles have been laid alternately on top of a concrete floor so that the planks run in two directions.

The cream painted shutters reflect light into the room and highlight the gold detail on the walls. To continue the look, add carved wooden furniture and dark wicker or bamboo storage baskets. Bamboo plants add to the eastern feel and a few carefully chosen ethnic artefacts such as the wicker plate above the bath make an unusual finishing touch. Add towels in neutral colours, such as soft beiges and creams, and brown and black accessories to add definition.

What else would work?

- stripped floorboards or wooden flooring
- neutral ethnic rugs
- plain walls

▲ Use straw or rattan rugs for a soft feel underfoot and to increase the Japanese effect.

▲ Carved wooden accessories work perfectly with the scheme and provide a lovely contrast to pale neutral colours.

▲ If ethnic wooden furniture proves too expensive, opt for natural wicker and rattan storage.

▲ Plants and pots of pebbles are an inexpensive way to add natural decoration suitable for this colour combination.

▲ A curvy chrome towel rail keeps towels neatly stored without taking up much space.

▲ A simple band of mosaic tiles adds colour and interest to plain walls.

Natural curves

This understated but stylish contemporary look is ideal for smaller bathrooms.

A D-shaped bath is ideal if you're short on space, and is a key feature of this look of curves and simple accents.

The pale colour scheme in this bathroom creates a feeling of space and light. White tiles will help to reflect light as well and are in keeping with this streamlined style. Paint the walls off white or a soft neutral shade like buttermilk and add a few simple bands of green mosaic tiles for accent colour and interest. The flooring imitates pale wood, but is easy to clean as it is made from vinyl.

In a really small room, make use of the space at the end of the bath by fitting a cabinet, which will also help to hide any unsightly pipework. Curvy, wave-shaped mirrors add interest and, again, enhance the light and space. If you can't find shaped mirrors, get them cut from a square mirror at a builder's merchant. Finally, add plants, green accessories and towels, along with touches of chrome and beech.

What else would work?

- neutral coloured flooring or carpet
- brass or gold instead of chrome
- beech accessories

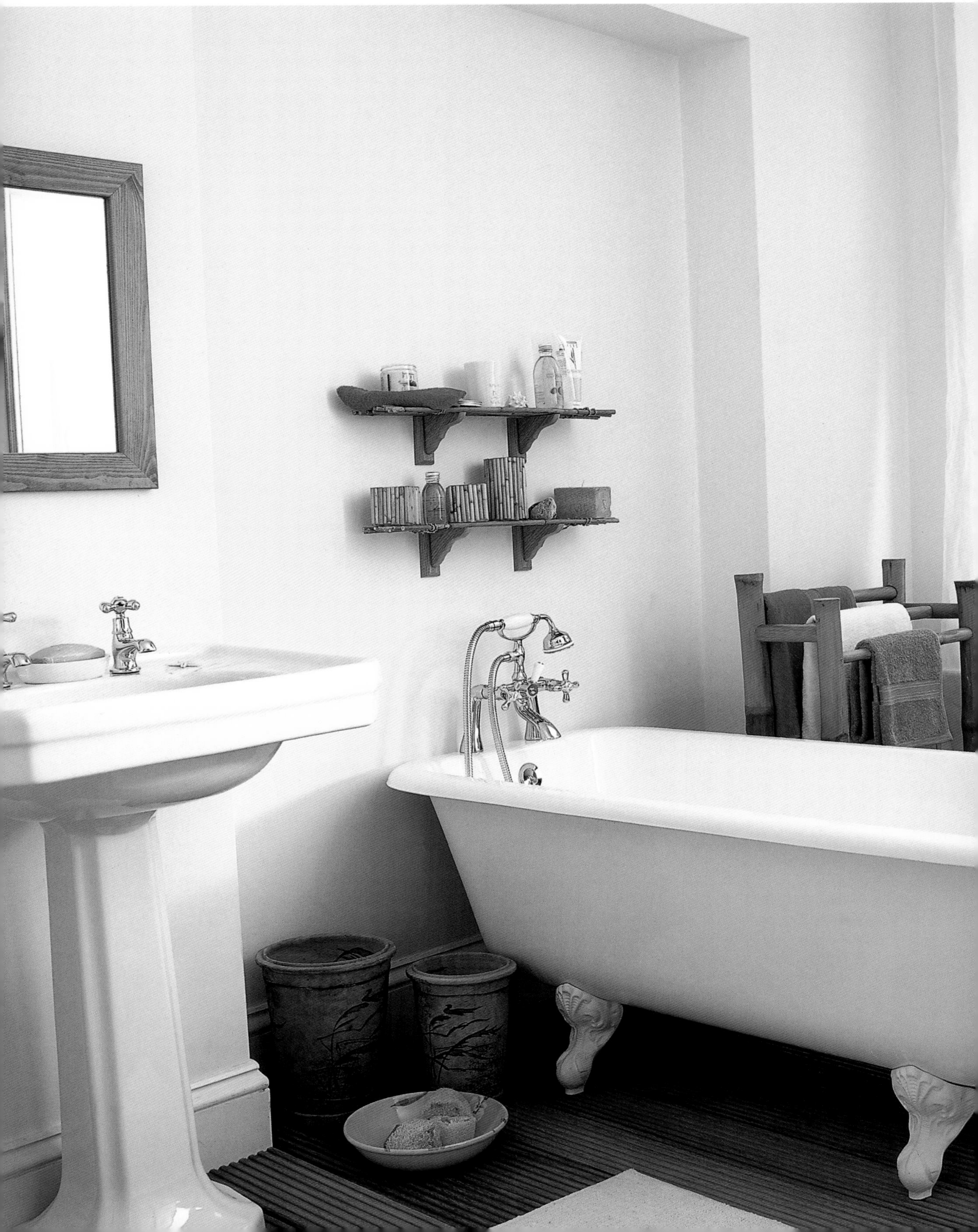

Back to nature

Create a calming oasis inspired by nature by combining bamboo, terracotta and creams.

This bathroom relies on rustic textures and natural materials to give it a warm feel. The roll-top bath is the focal point, matched by a traditional-style basin. The walls and the outside of the bath are painted cream, providing a subtle backdrop for the overall look.

The deep, cherry tone of the hardwood decking adds a wonderful richness to the overall scheme. Bamboo pieces are key to this look and shelves as well as accessories and a towel rail have been added to create a textural feel.

A wooden framed mirror above the sink is in keeping with the rich wood tones in this room. Accessories have been added in natural shades, such as cream and terracotta towels and rustic and soapstone bowls with a lovely natural finish. A sheer voile panel with a terracotta embroidered flower motif works with the colour scheme and adds just a simple touch of pattern to the room.

What else would work?

- any neutral bathroom suite
- ginger or terracotta walls
- paler wood floor and accessories

▲ Shelves made from natural products such as bamboo create an individual touch.

▲ Coloured towels add softness to this wood and rustic bathroom. Natural shades such as cream and terracotta add warmth and richness to the scheme.

▲ Decking adds rich colour to the room while providing a natural feel.

Natural Oriental

Add hints of Eastern style to your bathroom with bamboo, soft mint green shades and deck tiles.

A cream or white suite is always a good choice and can form the basis of numerous different styles. For a fresh and calming backdrop, use a soft mint green paint for the bathroom walls. A basic splashback is all that's needed – stick to cream or white tiles and add a few simple rows around the bath area and above the basin. For an instant update, lengths of bamboo have been fixed to the bath panel. These need to be tied with twine and fixed in place. The bamboo towel ladder also continues the theme.

Oriental-inspired motifs look great in this scheme. Here, simple picture panels have been painted on the walls, and a delicate leaf motif created in the centre of each one. Floorboards have been given a pale woodwash to add a pure and simple appeal to the room while decking tiles have been used as a bath mat. Keep accessories in just two or three toning colours to maintain the simplicity – here a soft lilac has been used for a touch of subtle contrast.

What else would work?

- cream floor tiles
- soft beige or fawn shades
- porcelain blue instead of mint green

▲ A towel ladder made of bamboo adds a rustic touch and provides an interesting, but practical, way to store towels.

▲ The bamboo theme running throughout the room adds a distinctive Oriental feel.

▲ A shower curtain with a leafy design gives this bathroom a subtle finishing touch.

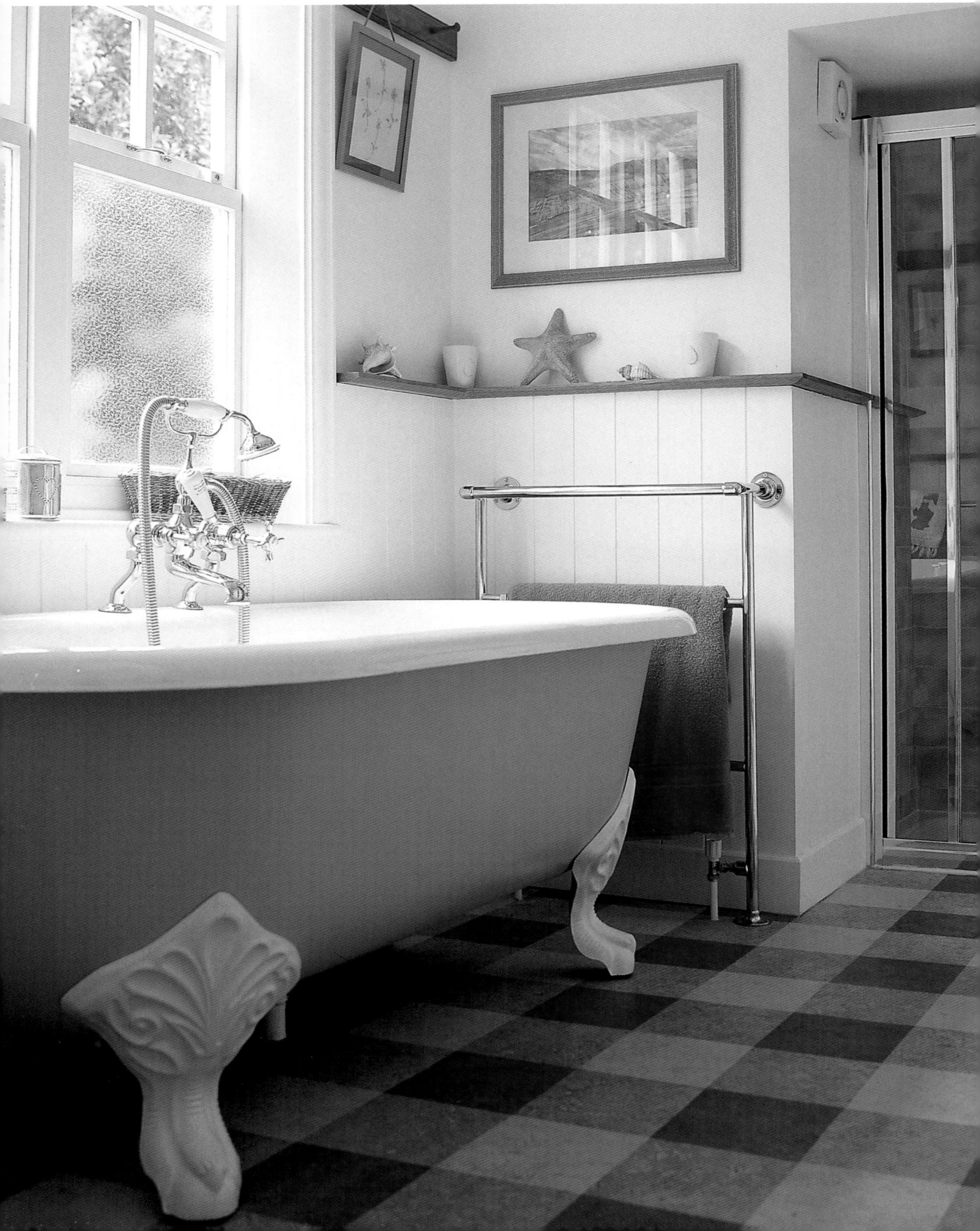

Shaker style

Give your bathroom a light and airy feel, taking inspiration from the practical Shaker style.

This airy bathroom incorporates several characteristic ingredients of the Shaker style. Start with a simple white suite – basic Victorian or Edwardian styles are perfect. Here, a classic roll-top bath adds character to the room and is finished with oatmeal paint on the outside. Walls are given a fresh and pure look with white paint, while wood panelling hints at Shaker style.

Natural materials are a key feature of the Shaker home – reflect this in the bathroom by keeping wood surfaces bare, except for a light stain or varnish. Furniture should be in a plain and simple design and, preferably, made of light woods. Peg rails are a classic feature of a Shaker look and can be used to hang bathroom accessories or even pictures. A chequered floor in natural shades provides subtle colour and adds interest. The essence of this look should be simple and uncluttered so use boxes or tins to keep everything stored away neatly.

What else would work?

- oatmeal carpet
- pale or white wood furniture
- deeper shades of terracotta or grey-green

▲ Keep surfaces simple. Adding a few key pieces, such as shells or plain candle-holders, is all you need to achieve this look.

▲ Painting the predominant areas in white or oatmeal will make the details in the room seem purer and more intense.

▲ Using patterned lino in subtle colours gives an impression of home-woven Shaker cloth.

Nautical style

A nautical theme is perfectly suited to a bathroom. It can be simplistic, sophisticated or fun. There is tremendous scope for many different nautical themes depending on the look and style you want to create – either go for the whole look or just add subtle echoes of the sea. Watery shades, from aquamarines to fresh, bold blues are the basis of this look. Nautical style can create a fun look for a family bathroom or a fresh, simple and stylish look in any home, modern or traditional.

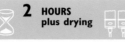
Seashore frame

A selection of beautiful seashells creates a decorative mirror frame.

1 Glue the four lengths wood together to make a frame, butting them up against each other on a work surface. The longer pieces form the top and bottom of the frame. Leave the glue to dry, then reinforce the joints at the back with mending plates.

2 To fit the hanging rope, make two marks on the top piece of the frame, equal distances from the sides, and drill a 1cm (⅜in) hole right through the frame at each mark.

2 HOURS plus drying

You will need
- two planks of softwood, about 40cm (16in) long
- two planks of softwood, about 30cm (12in) long
- wood glue
- steel mending plates
- screws
- screwdriver
- tape measure
- pencil
- drill
- paintbrush
- wood primer
- pale blue emulsion
- cream emulsion
- fine-grade sandpaper
- shells
- strong glue
- rope

3 Paint the frame with wood primer and allow to dry. Apply one coat of pale blue paint, leave to dry, then apply a wash of cream paint over the top of the blue. When dry, rub over the surface with fine-grade sandpaper until some blue shows through the cream.

4 Arrange the shells on the front of the frame and stick in place with strong glue. Thread the rope through the holes and secure with knots on either side at the front of the frame.

Mosaic stamped wall

Create the illusion of beautiful mosaic walls using a mosaic stamp and coloured paints.

1 Use a pencil to draw a grid of 2cm (¾in) squares on the foam. Cut away strips of foam in between the squares to leave just the 'tiles' standing proud. Paint the bathroom walls white and allow to dry.

2 Dab some white, light blue and dark blue paint on to a board or plate and blend them roughly together. Place the foam stamp in the paint mixture. Before you stamp directly on to the

  5 HOURS plus drying

You will need

- pencil
- ruler
- compacted foam rubber
- craft knife
- white emulsion paint
- paint brush
- light blue emulsion paint
- dark blue emulsion paint
- board or plate
- scrap paper

wall, practise on a piece of paper to help you get to grips with the amount of paint you need for the desired effect.

3 Once you are happy with your technique, start work on the wall. Begin at one side or the bottom edge of the wall to keep the design as straight and even as possible. Press the stamp firmly on to the wall, then carefully remove it and move on to the next patch. You may want to draw pencil guidelines on the wall to help you keep the lines straight. Repeat stamping until the whole area is covered. Leave to dry.

Shell tiles

Give plain tiles a fun, decorative touch by painting them with tile paints. Once they are painted, you can then fix them to the wall for a pretty border effect.

1 Painting your own tiles is easier than you think. As you will be painting freehand, it is a good idea to have an image (a photocopy, for example) to follow for each tile.

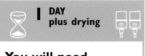

⏳ ❙ **DAY** plus drying

You will need
- copies of shell pictures
- white tiles
- tile paints, including white
- artist's paintbrushes

2 Paint the whole tiles carefully using a number of different coloured tile paints. A flat brush will help to give an even finish. You can paint some tiles with a different coloured border top and bottom, allowing the colours to merge together a little. Allow the paint to dry, following the manufacturer's instructions.

3 Use white paint to create the shell shapes, carefully following the copied images. Allow the paint to dry, then add details in a contrasting colour on top of the white. Allow to dry completely before fixing to the wall.

Denim curtain

This curtain treatment allows you to let in as much or as
little light as you like.

1 First measure the
window. Cut a piece of
denim to the same size,
adding an extra 5cm (2in)
to each side to allow for
hemming. Hem around the
fabric with blue cotton and
press. Turn the fabric to its
wrong side and mark out
the positions of the eyelets
with a pencil or tailor's
chalk, making sure they are evenly spaced.

2 Use an eyelet kit to fix eyelets around the fabric in the
places you have marked, working your way around the
blind. Fix nails along the top of the window frame,
making sure that they line up with the eyelet holes in the
fabric. Hang up the blind, by hooking the holes on to the
nails. You can move the eyelets to different hooks to
vary the way the blind falls.

2 HOURS

You will need
- tape measure
- denim (or other navy
  blue) fabric
- scissors
- sewing machine or
  needle and blue cotton
- pencil or tailor's chalk
- eyelet kit
- nails
- hammer

Glass splashback

A simple glass splashback will add a hint of green-aqua tones to your colour scheme, as well as giving a smart and stylish finish to the sink.

1 Measure the width of the back of your basin and get a piece of glass cut to size at a builder's merchant, asking them to make smooth curves on the top two corners. Put a piece of masking tape on the glass where you want to drill the holes to prevent the glass chipping or splintering. Drill the holes and remove the masking tape.

I HOUR

You will need
• wire-reinforced glass
• masking tape
• drill
• pencil
• wallplugs
• round-headed screws

2 Hold the splashback against the wall and make marks through the holes on the wall. Drill matching holes in the wall, put in wallplugs and screw the splashback in position. For a further coordinated look, you could also have a glass panel for your bath cut to size and apply it in the same way.

Woodwash stripes

Stripes give a floor a smart finish. Brush colourful woodwash on to alternate floorboards and seal with varnish for an effective and quick revamp.

1 Before painting floorboards they will need to be sanded to remove any old varnish and then cleaned thoroughly. Mask off alternate boards with masking tape and strips of newspaper.

DAY
plus drying

You will need
- masking tape
- newspaper
- blue woodwash
- paintbrush
- white woodwash
- quick-drying floor varnish

2 Shake the bottle of blue woodwash well and brush on to the naked boards, following the grain of the wood. Continue brushing along the whole length of each board to avoid overlapping marks.

3 Leave the blue boards to dry thoroughly, then remove the masking tape and newspaper. This time mask off the blue boards and paint the others with white woodwash in the same way.

4 Finally, once the boards are completely dry, apply several coats of floor varnish to protect them from wear and tear.

Frosted bathroom window

Transform a plain window into an elegant frosted panel, ideal for bathrooms where more privacy is needed.

1 Clean the window thoroughly, then mask off the area of the window you don't want to frost, using masking tape.

HOUR

You will need
- window cleaner
- cloth
- masking tape
- glass etch or frosting spray
- newspaper
- stencil (optional)

2 Practise with the etch spray on some newspaper before you spray the window, to familiarize yourself with the effect of the spray. Shake the can well before you begin. Avoid getting too close or the spray will be more likely to run.

3 Then, from a distance of 15–25cm (6–10in), spray the window with a coat of etch spray. Leave for five minutes to allow it to dry. Repeat with another coat. Leave to dry for 10 minutes and then peel off the masking tape. If you want to create a more decorative effect, cut out a stencil and use the cut-out piece on the window to create a pattern (the pattern will remain clear while the rest of the pane will be frosted).

Fresh tiles

Revamp your bathroom with new tiles – this blue and
white chequered design would work well with a nautical
theme. You can tile straight over the existing ones if they
are still firm.

1 Clean off any grease and
soap deposits from the
existing tiles and rake out
any loose grout from
between them.

2 Use a notched spreader
to spread tile adhesive
over a small area of tiles. It
is best to work on a small
area at a time to prevent
the adhesive from drying
out before you apply the tiles.

3 Carefully position one of the blue tiles on top and then
place a plain white one next to it. Use tile spacers
between the tiles to ensure even gaps. Repeat the
process until the whole area is covered. Leave for
48 hours for the adhesive to dry.

4 Remove the tile spacers. Fill the gaps between the tiles
with grout, then wipe the tiles clean with a damp cloth to
remove any excess grout.

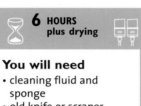

6 HOURS
plus drying

You will need
• cleaning fluid and
  sponge
• old knife or scraper
• tile adhesive and notched
  spreader
• blue tiles
• white tiles
• tile spacers
• tile grout
• damp cloth

Fresh touches

Wooden name pegs

This simple idea gives everyone their own personal space in the bathroom and adds a fun touch. Paint or varnish a peg rail or wooden plaque and leave to dry. Screw hooks into the plaque at even intervals. Fix brass label holders on to the peg rail or plaque and write labels with the names of each member of the family. Fasten in place on the wall.

45 MINUTES
plus drying

You will need
- peg rail or wooden plaque and screw-in hooks
- paint or varnish
- paintbrush
- brass label holders
- labels and pen
- drill
- wallplugs
- screws
- screwdriver

Towel trims

Cut two lengths of heavy, corded ribbon to fit the width of the towel. Pin the ribbon carefully in place, turning the raw edges under for a neat finish. Hand sew or machine stitch both sides to the towel.

30 MINUTES
per towel

You will need
- towel
- corded ribbon
- scissors
- pins
- sewing machine or needle and cotton

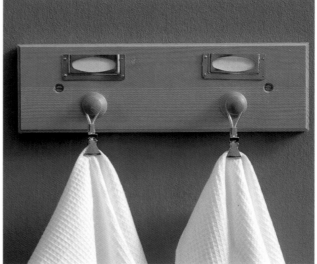

Shell and bead curtain

Cut some lengths of twine just over twice the depth of the window. Thread the beads and shells on to the twine, securing them with a knot below each one. Finish the ends with a bead, fastening the twine to itself around the bead.

 1 HOUR

You will need
- twine
- scissors
- glass beads
- shells
- bamboo cane
- 2 screw hooks

Tie the beaded twines in place on the bamboo cane, spacing them equally. Screw the hooks into the window frame and hang the cane in position.

Spotted cabinet doors

This simple trick creates a colourful and unusual effect. First paint the cabinet white, using an oil-based paint, and allow to dry.

2 HOURS
plus drying

You will need
- cabinet
- white oil-based paint
- paintbrush
- masking tape
- newspaper
- dark blue spray paint
- light blue spray paint

Mask off the areas around the door panels with masking tape and newspaper to ensure they are completely covered. Use the dark blue spray to make spots of colour on the panels, leaving enough space to add the light blue spots.

Allow to dry and repeat with the light blue paint. Allow to dry before removing the newspaper and masking tape.

Nautical motifs

Fishy border

Give plain ceramics a fishy theme using ceramic paint. Apply a strip of masking tape around the beaker about 2.5cm (1in) below the rim. Use a wide, flat paintbrush to paint the area above the tape with blue ceramic paint, aiming for a single, clean stroke around the beaker.

While the paint is still wet, use a sgraffito tool to scratch a number of fish motifs out of the blue paint. Allow to dry, then remove the masking tape.

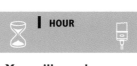

⧖ I HOUR

You will need
- masking tape
- wide, flat paintbrush
- blue ceramic paint
- sgraffito tool

Frosted toothbrush beaker

Stick paper hole reinforcers (available from stationery shops) on the outside of the glass to create the pattern. Spray the outside of the glass with frosting spray, holding the can 15–25cm (6–10in) away

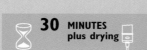

⧖ 30 MINUTES plus drying

You will need
- plain glass
- paper hole reinforcers
- glass etch or frosting spray

and aiming for an even coverage. Allow to dry and apply a second coat if necessary. When the paint is dry, remove the stickers.

Seashell window

Start by practising with the stencil and spray on some newspaper to master the technique. Then work out your design on the window, and fix the stencil to the window in the first position using spray adhesive. Use masking tape and newspaper to cover the areas surrounding the stencil, so the rest of the window doesn't get sprayed.

30 MINUTES

You will need
- shell stencil
- glass etch or frosting spray
- newspaper
- spray adhesive
- masking tape

Spray over the stencil to leave the shell pattern on the glass. Keep the spray 15–25cm (6–10in) away from the glass to avoid the spray running. Allow the spray to dry, then remove the stencil and newspaper and move on to the next motif, again covering the bulk of the window to prevent it getting sprayed. Repeat with the other motifs.

Bubble effect mural

Wash the surface with a mild detergent solution, and then wipe it over with a cloth rinsed in methylated spirit to remove any traces of grease. Make sure the surface is completely dry.

30 MINUTES

You will need
- mild detergent
- cloth
- methylated spirit
- tile transfer motifs
- scissors
- clean, lint-free cloth

For a neat finish, trim around each tile motif using sharp scissors, leaving just a small border of clear plastic around the design. Plan where you are going to position each motif before you stick any down.

Peel away the backing sheet of one of the motifs. Place the motif in position, then press it firmly in place using a clean, dry lint-free cloth to get rid of any air bubbles, working from the centre of the design to the outside edge. Avoid sticking the motifs in areas where they will become saturated (in a shower, for example).

Blue hues

Shades of blue, from pale to navy, aqua to cobalt, help to enhance the sea theme in a bathroom.

▲ Give mirror frames and toothbrush beakers a decorative mosaic trim in shades of blue.

▼ Make a laundry bag from a white towel and jazz it up with a smart checked fabric border. Use it for storing your laundry or even a bundle of clean towels.

▲ Blue flannels add a touch of vibrant colour in an otherwise white scheme. Tins with close-fitting lids will keep cotton wool or bath crystals dry. Give them a coat of white spray paint and glue on a motif cut from a wallpaper sample or giftwrap. Protect the paper with a coat of clear shellac varnish.

▲ Add a splash of colour to your scheme by fixing a length of blue towelling over a plain shower curtain. You could use a large beach towel – simply attach eyelets or sew ribbon ties along the top to attach to the shower curtain rail.

▲ Deep blue glass bowls can be used for storing soaps or decorative shells. Give a plain wood floor a subtle wash of watered-down white emulsion for a driftwood effect.

▲ Give an old unit, cupboard or chest of drawers a new look by painting it in an aqua shade. If it's melamine, use a melamine primer or suitable paint.

Seaside objects

Shells, driftwood and other seaside objects can add a wonderfully decorative element to your bathroom.

▲ Arrange seashells on a glass dish for a pretty bathroom display. Use a scallop shell as a soap dish.

▼ You can't beat a sheet of giftwrap for a budget print. With so many unusual designs available, you can either frame the whole page or cut out just one image or scene from the sheet.

▲ Give a glass lantern a seashell motif using a stencil and stencil paints. When lit it will cast wonderful patterns on to the walls.

▲ Display old household items such as galvanized metal jugs for a pretty and unusual decorative effect.

▲ Model sailboats add a fun decorative touch to a nautical scheme.

▲ Driftwood makes great decoration in a nautical bathroom. Use it on mirrors and frames or as decoration in its own right.

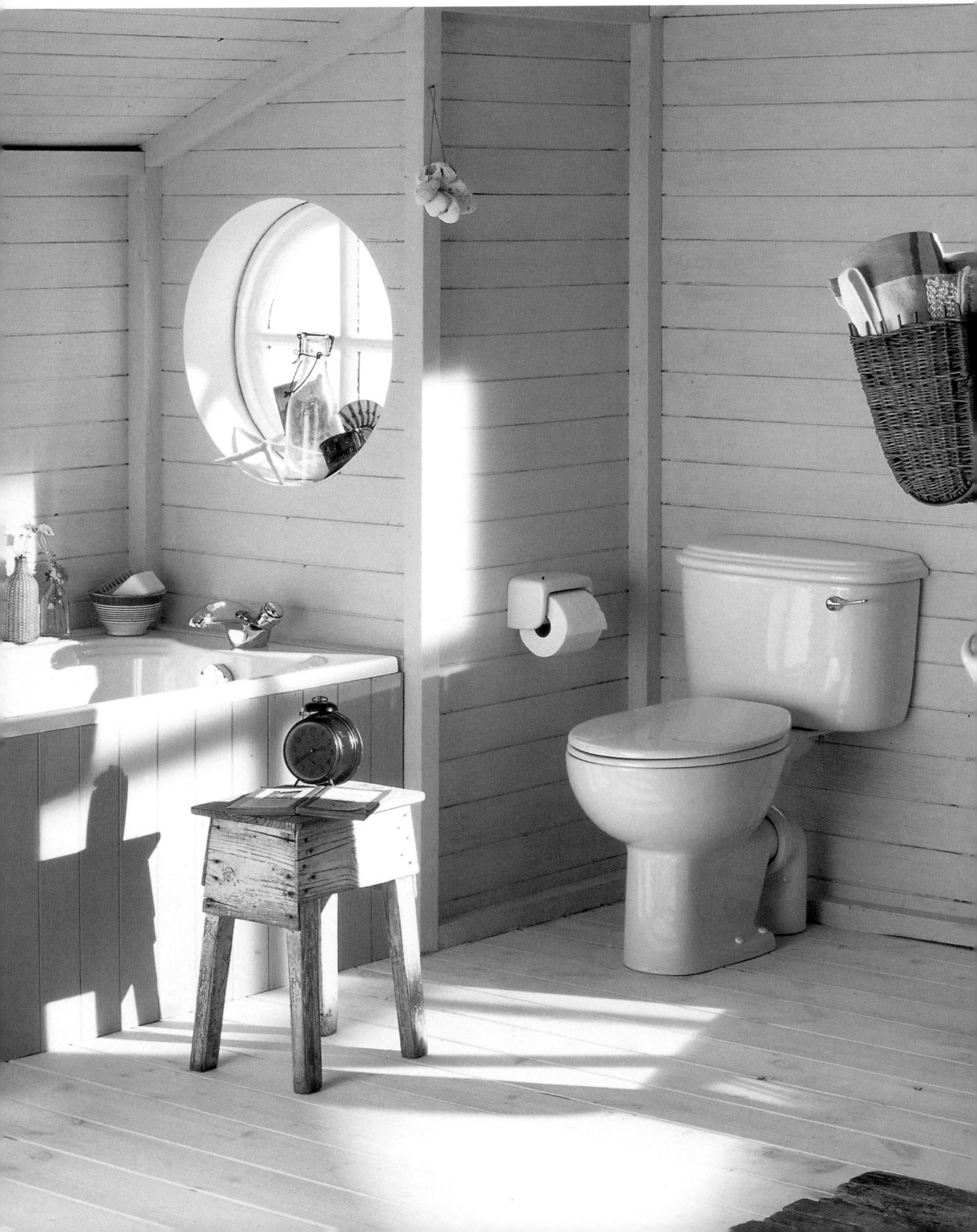

Beach hut

Create a beach hut in your own home with tongue-and-groove planks and objects from the seashore.

This rustic seaside bathroom is an easy look to create. Begin by covering the walls with tongue and groove, fixed horizontally. Don't worry about getting it too straight – a few gaps will add an authentic tone. Apply several coats of watered-down matt emulsion in an aqua shade. To carry this look through, add tongue-and-groove panelling to the bath panel, this time fixing it vertically. Paint or woodwash in the same way as the walls.

Wooden flooring or floorboards really help with the effect. Paint the boards a slightly paler shade of aqua, again watered down; add some white paint to the colour used for the walls to create a paler shade. Alternatively, use a white woodwash on an untreated wood floor.

Choose natural objects to decorate the room. A mirror framed in driftwood, rough wooden furniture and an assortment of shells and pebbles all help achieve the finished seaside look.

What else would work?

- white bathroom suite
- soft, pale blue walls
- rough painted wood furniture
- a deck chair

▲ A wavy rail made from decorative shelf trim adds to the seaside feel. Paint in a soft blue for a pretty decorative touch.

▲ A porthole window accentuates this look. If it is not possible to have one fitted, choose a porthole mirror as decoration.

▲ Decorate surfaces and shelves with blue and white china, seashells and wild flowers, to add a touch of colour.

Blue and white

Basic blue and white creates a fresh and clean feel. This is a very simple but effective look and is easy to achieve.

Begin by painting the bathroom walls in a milky white shade, then choose an area of wall to decorate, such as the top half. Create your own wallpaper design using a stamp. Pick a simple shape such as a basic flower and a fresh sea blue shade of stamp paint or matt emulsion. Use the stamp motif to add lines or rows of colour to create an overall pattern. If you are covering a large area mark the rows on the wall first using a pencil and ruler.

Take a basic white or cream roman blind and decorate it with small fabric squares to tie in with your colour scheme. Denim or gingham is perfect for this look. Attach the fabric to the blind with iron-on hem tape, or alternatively use a needle and cotton. Paint floorboards with soft, milky white, oil-based paint or woodwash. Finally, add a few blue accessories to hold the scheme together.

What else would work?

- blue and white gingham blind or curtain
- neutral coloured carpet
- nautical stripes on the walls

▲ Use wood as an accent to give the scheme warm tones. Add touches with items such as bath racks, chests and accessories.

▲ Line shelves with jars of coloured bath salts and soaps to create a colourful but orderly display, in keeping with the strong blue and white scheme.

▲ Decorative frames and mirrors painted in blue add a touch of pattern to this simple look.

Country style

There is a great diversity of looks you can give your bathroom to create a country style. Accessories and key pieces help to complete this look and you really can have fun building a scheme – be as eclectic or as simple as you want. Unusual furniture and objects, as well as more traditional pieces, add strength and character. A country look works perfectly in bathrooms with traditional features but a more modern bathroom can also be given a country feel with carefully chosen furnishings.

Ribbon-tied blind

Ribbon ties enhance this tailor-made blind to create a pretty window treatment. Choose a checked ribbon to coordinate with the curtain fabric.

1 Cut a rectangle of fabric to fit the window, allowing an extra 2cm (¾in) all round for hems. Hem the fabric on all sides using iron-on hem tape.

2 Cut two lengths of checked ribbon, each twice as long as the drop of the blind. Fold the two ribbons in half and stitch them to the top of the blind by their mid points, allowing half of the ribbon to hang down the front and half down the back of the blind.

3 Attach the blind to the window frame using self-adhesive touch-and-close tape, so that the blind can be removed for cleaning. Gather up the fabric and tie the ribbons into bows underneath the blind to hold it in place.

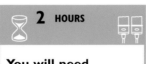

⏳ **2 HOURS**

You will need

- fabric
- tape measure
- scissors
- iron-on hem tape
- iron
- checked ribbon
- needle and cotton
- self-adhesive touch-and-close tape

Handy shelving unit

For a clutter-free bathroom, transform a plain wooden clothes airer into a practical open storage unit. Use a patterned waterproof fabric to cover each shelf.

1 Open out the airer and measure the dimensions for the shelves, adding an extra 3cm (1¼in) to the depth to allow some overhang. Get a sheet of 6mm (¼in) MDF cut to size for the shelves.

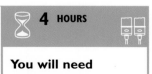

4 HOURS

You will need
- clothes airer
- tape measure
- sheet of 6mm (¼in) MDF cut to size
- 12mm (½in) battening
- wood glue
- panel pins
- waterproof fabric
- staple gun

2 Cut two pieces of batten to the same length as each shelf. Glue one on each long edge and secure with panel pins. These will prevent the shelves moving around.

3 Cut a piece of fabric to fit each shelf, allowing an extra 10cm (4in) all round for overlap. Carefully staple the overlapping fabric in place on the undersides of each shelf, stretching it to ensure you create a flat surface. Sit the shelves in position on the airer.

Revamped floorboards

Transform plain floorboards with a coat of pale paint and add a simple border around the room for definition.

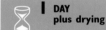

☙ I DAY plus drying

You will need
- low-tack masking tape
- pale floor paint
- roller or synthetic paintbrush
- soft pencil
- long ruler
- dark floor paint

1 Make sure the floor is thoroughly free of all traces of dirt, dust or grease. Use low-tack masking tape to protect the skirting boards and door frames from paint splashes.

2 Apply two coats of pale floor paint using a roller or a synthetic paintbrush, allowing at least 4 hours between coats for the paint to dry.

3 When the paint has dried completely, draw the border straight on to the floor using a soft pencil and a ruler. Mask off the outline, including the outer lines, with low-tack masking tape.

4 Fill in the border in the darker paint, taking care not to paint beyond the masking tape. Before the paint dries, peel off the tape. Allow the floor to dry completely.

Lace door cabinet

Add a pretty, lace screen door to a shelf unit to hide the bathroom clutter inside.

1 Cut two lengths of hardwood to the height of the unit, and two pieces to the width of the unit minus 20cm (8in). Sand the ends to remove any splinters, then glue them together to make a doorframe.

2 When the glue is dry, screw mending plates across the joins of the wood inside of the door. Fix the doorknob on to the outside of the door and then paint the door with primer and allow to dry.

4 HOURS
plus drying

You will need
- plain wood shelving unit
- hardwood batten, 10cm (4in) wide and 12mm (½in) thick
- sandpaper
- wood glue
- mending plates
- screws
- screwdriver
- doorknob
- wood primer
- paintbrush
- oil-based paint
- lace fabric
- needle and cotton
- upholstery tacks
- hammer
- 2 hinges
- pencil
- drill

3 Lightly sand the shelving unit inside and out and paint with primer. Leave to dry, then paint both the door and the unit with coloured oil-based paint. Allow to dry.

4 Hem the fabric on all four edges and fix it on to the back of the door using upholstery tacks. Hold the door in place on the unit and mark where you want to position the hinges on the frame and unit. Drill holes and screw the hinges into place.

Pretty touches

Aged frame

Rub the candle over the corners and edges of the frame. The paint will not stick to these areas.

Paint the frame blue. When dry, rub the candle over the frame in a few places. Apply a coat of off-white emulsion. When dry, sand until areas of wood show and varnish the frame.

Drill two small holes in each side of the frame, about 1cm (⅜in) apart. Thread wire though them, around the test tubes and twist to secure at the back. Fill the tubes with water and flowers.

3 HOURS plus drying

You will need
- mirror with untreated wooden frame
- candle
- blue emulsion paint
- paintbrush
- off-white emulsion paint
- sandpaper
- matt varnish
- drill
- galvanized wire
- 2 test tubes

Poppy tie-back

Wind a length of garden twine around the curtain, making sure you don't pull too tight, and fasten in a knot at the back. Decorate with an artificial bloom, such as a poppy.

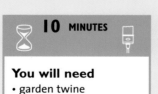

10 MINUTES

You will need
- garden twine
- scissors
- artificial flower

Silver bucket

Remove all traces of dirt, grease and grime from a plain enamel bucket with soap and a damp cloth. Sit the bucket on a large amount of newspaper to protect the surrounding area. Shake the can well and spray the bucket with gentle sweeping movements, from left to right. Be careful not to use the spray too close to the bucket, otherwise the paint will run. Leave to dry and apply another coat if needed. Once dry, fill with flowers to make a pretty corner feature.

 15 MINUTES plus drying

You will need
- enamel bucket
- soap and damp cloth
- newspaper
- silver or chrome spray paint

Country table

If your table has any varnish or paint on it, give it a good sanding then move straight on to the oil-based paint. If the wood is untreated, paint it with wood primer and allow to dry. Next apply a coat of oil-based paint with the roller and leave to dry.

Rub the corners of the   table, including the legs, with the sandpaper to expose patches of bare wood. Use the same technique on other parts of the table at random. Then wipe the table with a damp cloth to remove any dust.

2 HOURS plus drying

You will need
- wood furniture
- sandpaper
- wood primer (optional)
- paintbrush
- oil-based paint such as satinwood
- mini paint roller
- damp cloth

Subtle decoration

Hook panel

Mark a panel on the wall where your hooks are going to be, using a ruler and pencil. Check the lines are straight with a spirit level. Mask the area outside the lines with masking tape.

Paint the panel in your chosen colour and allow the paint to dry. Drill holes in the panel where the hooks are going to go and insert wallplugs. Screw the hooks in place.

⧗ **I HOUR** plus drying 🖌

You will need
- ruler
- pencil
- spirit level
- masking tape
- paint
- paintbrush
- decorative hooks
- drill
- wallplugs
- screws
- screwdriver

Edged towels

Cut a piece of ribbon and two pieces of lace edging to the width of the towel. Pin them in place about 10cm (4in) from one end of the towel, with the lace poking out from under the ribbon on each side. Carefully sew the trimmings in place and then remove the pins.

⧗ **45 MINUTES** per towel 🖌

You will need
- plain towel
- wide patterned ribbon
- lace edging
- scissors
- pins
- sewing machine or needle and cotton

Mosaic and shell vase

Liven up glass pots and vases by decorating them with glass mosaic tiles and shells. The glass tiles will give the vase a lovely translucent quality which is ideal for candle-holders.

Use a spatula to apply a thick, even coat of tile adhesive to the vase, then carefully stick on the tiles. As you do so, place decorative shells at random points between the tiles. Once dry, apply grout between the tiles to finish.

2 HOURS per pot

You will need
- tile nippers
- ceramic tiles
- spatula
- tile adhesive
- decorative shells
- tile grout

Shower curtain cover

Measure your existing shower curtain and cut a piece of fabric to the same size, allowing extra for hems. Hem the fabric all round to prevent fraying.

Fix eyelets at equal intervals along the top edge, then add shower curtain hooks and hang the fabric in front of your shower curtain.

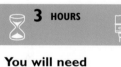

3 HOURS

You will need
- tape measure
- gingham fabric
- scissors
- needle and cotton
- eyelet kit
- shower curtain hooks

Sweet features

Give your bathroom a few pretty features by customizing objects and adding quick decoration. Use organza fabrics for a softening effect and liven up plain ceramics with colourful floral designs. Flowers and plants also make good finishing touches.

▼ A two-tier table provides storage for towels and laundry as well as a surface for decorative objects.

▲ Customize plain ceramics with a simple flower motif. Paint on freehand or try using a stencil.

▲ Aged and weathered items add charm to any bathroom and a collection of old crackled ceramic vases will make a pretty display.

▲ Make a sachet from a sheer fabric such as organza.
Fill it with aromatic herbs and tie with a ribbon to give a
sweetly scented decorative touch.

▲ Paint an old galvanized bucket with high gloss
enamel and hang from a peg rail as a stylish plant pot.

▲ Silk flowers add a romantic feel to a bathroom.
Arrange them in vases or tuck behind mirrors.

Country materials

Make sure your bathroom has a few rustic touches for a country-style look – use natural materials in creative ways.

▼ Make tealight holders from small branches of wood by drilling or carving several holes in the top large enough to hold a tealight.

▲ Use decorative wooden boxes for storing make-up and toiletries.

▲ Hang wooden accessories and frames from rough twine for that authentic country look.

▲   Wire baskets make a pretty feature for storing make-up, pots and jars. Choose galvanized wire to counteract the steam in the bathroom.

▲   Enamel buckets placed in a row and hooked to the wall make an unusual but handy storage feature.

▲   An elegant wooden ladder can be given a new lease of life as simple, but useful towel rail.

American country style

Give your bathroom a country look with hints of Shaker style, using plain, country furniture and muted colours.

Begin by choosing a muted shade of paint for the scheme – opt for sage green, dusky blue or rich cream. Fix simple, unfussy wood panelling to the walls, and then paint, covering walls, window frames and doors in the same shade. Choose gingham or checked fabrics in green, blue or yellow to make curtains, blinds and a fabric door panel. Hook curtain wires across the top and bottom of the door panel and thread them through channels in the fabric panel.

A dark wooden floor is perfectly suited to this look. Another key element is the peg rail – it is practical and creates the right effect. Use one or more to hang decorative items and more functional pieces, such as mirrors and bathroom accessories. Finally, add some simple furniture in either dark wood or painted the same colour as the walls. A checked rug completes the look.

What else would work?

- plain walls instead of panelling
- muted blue paint
- heart motifs
- dark wood furniture

▲ Peg rails provide a functional element and ensure that the room stays free of clutter.

▲ Decorate shelves and windowsills with jugs of dried flowers to give a rural touch.

▲ Use gingham fabric as a decorative element. It also works well on cupboard doors and storage jars or tins.

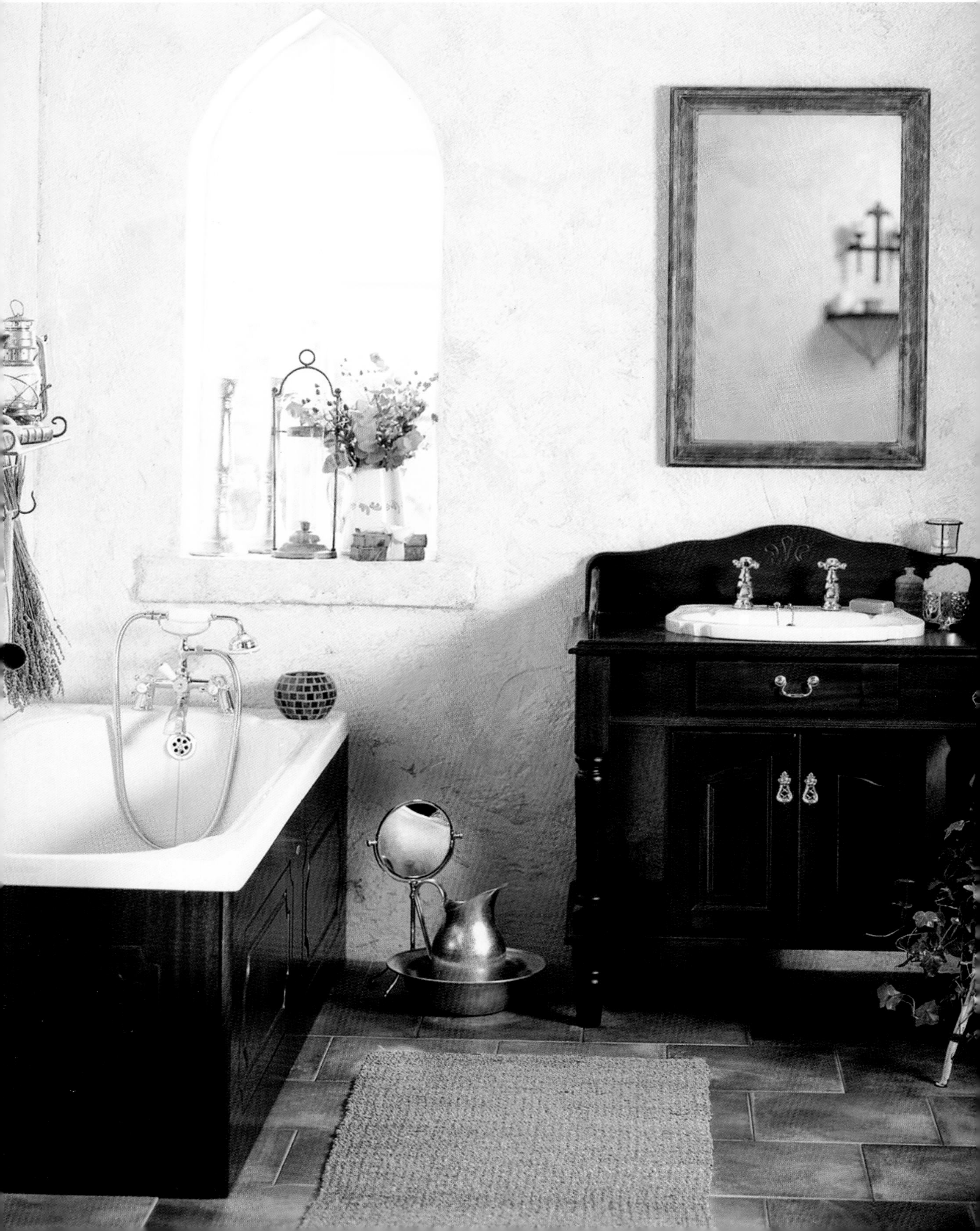

A touch of Provençe

Textured walls, dark wood and ironwork create a cosy and individual look.

Start by adding rough plaster or a textured paint to give the walls a rustic finish. Alternatively, you could paint smooth walls with a broken colourwash to create a similar effect. Choose a warm cream, and highlight the textural effect with a fawn shade.

This look relies on individual pieces of furniture in dark wood, such as the free-standing basin unit. You could transform existing pieces using a dark varnish or woodstain to achieve the same effect. Choose similar wood for the bath panel and give it a dark woodstain or varnish. Stone flooring echoes the rustic feel of this bathroom – here it has been finished with sisal matting.

Choose ironwork shelves for the walls and add hooks to hang unusual items. Finish with plants and flowers to echo the country theme. Look for finishing touches from the outdoors – perhaps a garden chair and ironwork furniture if you've got the room.

What else would work?

- colourwashing smooth walls
- warm, earthy shades such as golden yellow, orange or terracotta
- ironwork furniture instead of wood

▲ To bring the great outdoors inside, display bushy plants.

▲ Look out for old watering cans and enamel buckets. If they are too badly worn, spray them with a fresh coat of paint.

▲ Ironwork gives an unusual decorative touch and can be added through small accessories or larger pieces of furniture.

▲ Decorative items should be kept to a minimum, so make a feature of any you do use.

▲ Choose a few accessories in natural materials such as wood, stone or bamboo.

▲ A simple, but decorative addition, such as a plaque, will add a point of interest and can be painted in a pale shade to blend in with the walls.

Pure and simple

This simple but stylish look relies on very limited colour and tones – texture is all.

Choose a soft milky white colour for your bathroom walls and add very simple panelling, if desired, painted in the same shade. Paint the skirting, window frames and doors in the same colour.

Don't break the effect with a different colour on the floor. Try either painting existing floorboards with the same shade of colour as the walls or, if floorboards are new or in good enough condition, a white woodwash works perfectly to give a slightly more 'raw' feel. The woven rug provides a change of texture but blends seamlessly with the room's overall colouring.

Dress the window with a simple blind or curtain made from a natural fabric like calico or muslin. Another key feature is the lack of furniture and accessories. Any that you add should be kept to a minimum; look out for accessories made from natural materials such as stone and keep the furniture simple, fuss-free and, most important of all, white.

What else would work?

- simple patterned blind or curtain in neutral colours
- chrome or brass bath fittings
- textured cream carpet or flooring

Country cottage

This bathroom is simple and inexpensive to create. It relies on dainty floral patterns and soft pastels which work perfectly in a smaller bathroom, giving it an intimate and cosy feel.

A classic suite will really set the scene, but this look can easily be created around a standard white suite. Old-fashioned, classic fittings, in gold, brass or chrome help to give this room its character.

Panel the walls with tongue and groove up to the dado rail and give them a coat of cream or buttermilk paint. For the walls above the panelling, choose a classic, dainty floral paper. This paper can even be continued over the ceiling for maximum effect. Choose simple off-white tiles, but don't go overboard with them, just use them where they are really needed. Choose pretty floral curtains for the windows, to carry through the cottage theme. Accessories such as a vase of flowers, a rustic stool and a cotton bath rug are perfect as finishing touches.

What else would work?

- painted pastel walls with a floral stamped motif
- pastel coloured carpet
- using wallpaper on just one wall

▲ Decorative corner shelves add a discreet but pretty feature, while providing extra storage at the same time. Paint them to blend in with the general colour scheme.

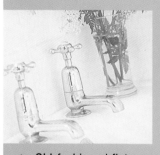

▲ Old-fashioned fixtures including tap fittings really enhance the cottage theme, while a simple vase of flowers adds a delicate and pretty touch.

▲ Choose old-fashioned floral fabrics to create classic curtains for a pretty and cosy feel.

Index

Acknowledgements

The publisher wishes to thank the organizations listed below for their kind permission to reproduce the photographs in this book. Every effort has been made to acknowledge the picture properly, however we apologize if there are any unintentional omissions which will be corrected in future editions.

All pictures are copyright of The National Magazine Company Limited, except for the following listed below:

Armitage Shanks /stockists tel: 01543 490 253/ www.armitage-shanks.co.uk 7 top right 7 top left, 8, 11 right, 12 bottom, 13 Top, 15 bottom left, 63 top left.
Cath Kidston Ltd /stockists tel: 020 7221 4000/ www.cathkidston.co.uk 104 top left 112 top left, 115 right.
Contour /stockists tel: 01670 718 300 9 top, 14 top centre, 14 top right, 24 top left, 38 top left, 54–55, 55 top right, 55 centre right, 55 bottom right.
Crown Paints /stockists tel: 01254 704 951/ www.crownpaint.co.uk 30 bottom left 82 bottom right, 97 bottom left.
Croydex Group plc /stockists tel: 01264 365 881 18 bottom left, 27 bottom right.
Dolphin Bathrooms /stockists tel: 0800 626 717www.dolphinbathrooms.com 7 bottom 10, 36 top left, 36 centre left, 36 bottom left, 36–37, 52–53, 53 top right, 53 centre right, 53 bottom right.
Dulux /stockists tel: 01753 550 555/ www.dulux.co.uk 12 top.
Eclectics /stockists tel: 01843 852 888/ www.eclectics.co.uk 18 top left 19, 30 bottom right, 31 bottom left.
H&R Johnson Ltd /stockists tel: 01782 575 575/ www.johnson-tiles.com 24 bottom right.
Homebase /stockists tel: 0870 900 8098/ www.homebase.co.uk 104 top right, 114 top left.
Ideal Standard Ltd/tel: 01482 346 461/ www.ideal-standard.co.uk 9 bottom 34–35, 35 top right, 35 centre right, 35 bottom right, 72–73, 73 top right, 73 centre right, 73 bottom right, 82 top left, 100–101, 101 top right, 101 centre right, 101 bottom right.
International Paints /stockists tel: 01962 717 001/ www.international-paints.co.uk 11 left 97 bottom right, 99 right, 108 top left, 108 centre, 108 bottom.
Octopus Publishing Group Limited 125 top right, /Peter Myers back cover left, 66 bottom left, 69 bottom left, 80–81, 81 top right, 81 centre right, 81 bottom right, /Polly Wreford 124–125, 125 centre right, 125 bottom right.
Porcelanosa /stockists tel: 0800 915 4000. 26 top left.
Qualceram Shires Bathrooms /stockists tel: 01274 523 366/ www.qualceram-shires.com 120–121121 top right, 121 centre right, 121 bottom right.
Readyroll /stockists tel: 01670 718 300 95 top left.
Trent Bathrooms /stockists tel: 01782 202 334/ www.trent-bathrooms.co.uk 122 top left, 122 centre left, 122 bottom left, 122–123.
Visions /stockists tel: 01274 521 199/ www.visions-bathrooms.co.uk 118–119, 119 top right, 119 centre right, 119 bottom right.
Wickes /(tel: 0500 300 328) 31 right.
Woolworths /(stockists tel: 01706 862 789) 15 top left, 38 bottom left, 41 right, 41 top left.

Executive Editor: Anna Southgate
Editor: Rachel Lawrence
Executive Art Editor: Leigh Jones

Designer: Claire Harvey
Picture Researcher: Zoë Holtermann
Your Home **Picture Coordination:** Jill Morgan

Production Controller: Jo Sim